Always Be
your Very
Best!

Lee Milteer

MORE PRAISE FOR *FEEL AND GROW RICH* :

"Money really *isn't* everything. In *Feel and Grow Rich*, Lee Milteer redefines wealth for the motivated masses—and shows you how to tap some of the riches of information, knowledge and energy you already have inside."

—Curtis Pesmen
Author, *What She Wants: A Man's Guide to Women*, Health & Features Editor, *Self Magazine*

"Inspiring. Contains more truth on living a successful life than any book I've seen. It's a must read!"

—Ted Nicholas
Author, *How To Publish A Book and Sell A Million Copies*

"Lee Milteer has written a wonderful, witty, thought-provoking and inspiring book on how to achieve greater success and happiness in the human experience. It should be read and re-read by anyone who is seriously interested in being happier and more effective in their personal and business life."

—Brian Tracy
Author, *Maximum Achievement*

"*Feel and Grow Rich* is a page-turner that stimulates new possibilities instantly. I love it and recommend it to everyone who wants to be more, do more, and have more."

—Mark Victor Hansen
Author, *Dare to Win* and co-author, *Chicken Soup for the Soul*

"Every entrepreneur, executive and salesperson can instantly profit from this information. With it, you CAN inspire yourself to get anything you want. I recommend it enthusiastically!"

—Dan Kennedy
Author, *The Ultimate No BS, No Holds Barred, Kick Butt, Take No Prisoners And Make Tons Of Money Business Success Book*, Entrepreneur, Consultant and Speaker

"What a great book for anyone who seeks to grow successfully and enjoy life joyously. Easy to read. Practical. Packed with wisdom and inspiration. Highly recommended."

—Nido R. Qubein
Chairman, Creative Services, Inc.

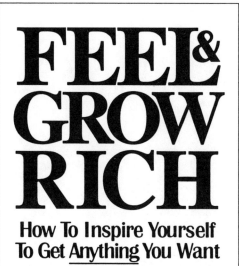

FEEL& GROW RICH

How To Inspire Yourself To Get Anything You Want

Lee Milteer

HAMPTONROADS PUBLISHING COMPANY, INC.

Hampton Roads Publishing Company, Inc.
891 Norfolk Square
Norfolk, Virginia 23502
Or call: (804) 459-2453
FAX: (804) 455-8907

If you are unable to order this book from your local
bookseller, you may order directly from the publisher.
Call 1-800-766-8009, toll free.

Cover design by Patrick Smith

ISBN 1-878901-88-5

10 9 8 7 6 5 4 3 2 1

Printed on acid-free paper in the United States of America

Dedication

This book is dedicated to my parents,
Esther and Horace Milteer

ACKNOWLEDGMENTS

I would like to thank all those who helped make this book possible. In particular, Bob Friedman and all the great people at Hampton Roads Publishing for believing in me and my work. I want to acknowledge and thank Wanda Newman, my personal assistant, for her positive reinforcement and the tireless hours of hard work during office hours plus evenings and weekends of typing and editing. I also want to thank my assistants, Patty Ehlers and Cindy Mayo, for their support and the work they did to make this book possible. A special thanks to Deborah Taylor for helping me to get started writing on my own. I want to acknowledge Ted Nicholas for his help with the book title; Dan Kennedy, Jeff Herman, and Jess Stearn for believing in me and encouraging me to keep writing.

I want to acknowledge and thank my family for their love and support: my parents, Esther and Horace Milteer; my brother Gray, his wife Holly, and their children, Rachel and Gray.

I would also like to express appreciation to my extended family for their love, support, and encouragement: Clif Williams, Sally Perry, Bill Anderson, Graham Stronge, Sue Paro, Caroline and Michael McCartney, Michael Myers, Earlene Grant, Sue Krusa, Roger Mellott, Claudia Ross, Phyllis Higginbottem, Mary and Andy Nichols, Tim Smith, and Sharon Culpepper.

And finally, many blessings to all my clients and customers for their trust in my material.

TABLE OF CONTENTS

FOREWORD / xi

CHAPTER 1 / 1
Take Back Your Life

CHAPTER 2 / 6
**How To Ask Questions
To Improve The Quality Of Your Life**

CHAPTER 3 / 15
**How To Find Your Talents
And Capitalize On Them**

CHAPTER 4 / 28
Success Self-Programming

CHAPTER 5 / 42
Your Declaration Of Independence

CHAPTER 6 / 60
Dream Big—Become A Visonary

CHAPTER 7 / 73
Intuition—Your Secret Talent

CHAPTER 8 / 88
Capitalizing On Change

CHAPTER 9 / 103
Developing The Entrepreneurial Spirit

CHAPTER 10 / 118
**Creating Prosperity Regardless
Of The Economy**

CHAPTER 11 / 142
**Redefining Wealth—Determine
What Success Means To You**

CHAPTER 12 / 154
**How To Plug Energy Leaks That
Hold You Back From Success**

CHAPTER 13 / 169
**Face Your Dragons And Win
The Game Of Life**

CHAPTER 14 / 178
Build An Emotional Foxhole For Tough Times

CHAPTER 15 / 186
Enjoy Life! This Is Not A Dress Rehearsal

CHAPTER 16 / 194
**How To Project Confidence
And Promote Yourself**

CHAPTER 17 / 215
Designing Your Destiny

CHAPTER 18 / 237
The 21-Day Success Fitness Plan

A PERSONAL AFTERWORD / 249

RESOURCES / 251

FOREWORD

You have within you unlimited potential to create the quality of life that you want. One of the most important resources you have available to you is the ability to tap into your feelings. You must *feel* your power before you can take your vision, your hopes, and your fantasies and make them real. All success must be created internally before it can be created externally. This book will give you the information, philosophies, skills, and strategies that will assist you in empowering yourself to make the changes you desire most in order to create a *rich* life.

This is not just a book about money; it's about the quality of life that you lead, using your life energy efficiently, and living your life with integrity, reflecting your values.

The idea for this book began when I started to realize that *thinking* alone would not make me (or anyone) successful. Our society teaches us how to think but not how to feel. We have been programmed to be logical and analytical in our thinking to the point that we have almost forgotten the intuitive, creative part of ourselves—our feelings. Since yesterday's programming cannot solve all of today's challenges or allow us to capitalize on new opportunities, we must create our own destinies by learning to listen to our inner selves and by using our inborn talents.

One of the biggest secrets of life is that you must *feel* successful before you can create it in your outer world. Our emotions create our behaviors; our behaviors create our results and successes. Our lives are driven by our emotions and how we feel about ourselves and the world.

After years of presenting seminars around the world, I have observed that you can give people all the proven external techniques and strategies for success in any field, but if they don't *feel* they can do them, they won't. We are self-fulfilling prophecies. Our feelings determine what we aspire to be and what we can accomplish in life. Our feelings will determine how many calculated risks we will take and how confident we are in any endeavor. Depending only on our thinking abilities will leave us lacking in motivation, passion, and excitement. Without the essential ingredients of *feeling* powerful we will not muster the necessary energy to inspire ourselves to go for our dreams and goals.

This book will offer you specific, measurable strategies to move past old limitations and create skills to increase the quality of your life. Life in today's world holds an infinite number of possibilities for you to apply your talents in ways of which you may never have dreamed. But first, you have to feel you have the power to write your own life script. By taking responsibility for your feelings you choose to be proactive in life and not just let life happen to you. This book will help you enlarge the repertoire of the resources you have to become prosperous. These principles will transform your life into richness by expanding your boundaries to claim for yourself new territories of the mind and spirit.

_1_

TAKE BACK YOUR LIFE

Remember when you were a kid, and you used to dream about the day you would be in charge of your destiny and nothing could stop you from being exactly what you wanted to be? Now, as an adult, you have the authority you wished for as a child. But are things going the way you had planned? Does your life seem to be all work and no play? Do you feel uneasy about your future or anxious about your job security? Have you given up your hopes and dreams without realizing it? Are you getting the sense of gratification that you had hoped for? For many of us, the dream of that great life has somehow faded away.

From childhood, we've been taught to do what authority figures told us to do. We have been programmed that other people are smarter and wiser and have more experience. We've been warned about the disastrous results that might happen if the rules aren't followed. The bottom line is that we've been taught to give our power away and not trust our own judgment and our feelings.

Without even realizing it, we have given away our power to live the rich lives that we deserve. We stay in jobs that we hate—hanging in there because of a dental plan or retirement in eleven years, trading satisfaction and fulfillment for an illusion of security. We hold onto relationships that have been dead for years, for the sake of the children or outside appearances. Many of us have turned over so much authority to our spouses that a good portion of our married lives is spent resenting them for treating us like children! Time is too often devoted to old traditions we dislike but continue to follow, surrendering our personal preferences.

We give away peace of mind to our internal fears and doubts when it's time to take risks or change our lives. We give away our power to enjoy the present whenever we worry about the future or feel guilty about the past.

Think how easily negative people ruin our day. There is loss in forfeiting our power of choice to the bevy of professionals to whom we've turned over our affairs, such as lawyers, accountants, and financial advisors. Many times we do not even question doctors who may perform unnecessary operations or prescribe drugs creating side effects that do us more harm than good.

We've been so trained to be the caretakers of others that, when we think about dealing with our own needs and acting on our feelings, we suddenly feel we are being selfish. How dare we put life enjoyment above hard work? How dare we think only of ourselves? Many times if we do start to think about our needs and wants, we suffer the fear that we will be seen as egomaniacs and self-centered.

We often lose touch with our own personal needs and feelings if we monitor other people's feelings for our own sense of who we are and how we're doing. In effect, we're measuring our insides by other people's outsides! When we're in tune with our own needs and accept ourself as individuals, we don't need to monitor others for a sense of self. We do not need to be all things to all people—which is a good thing because no one can!

It's Time to Take Back Your Life!

The truth is that meeting your own needs is a basic survival technique for having a successful, happy, and rich life. You have only so much mental, physical, emotional, and spiritual life energy. If you use all your energy serving the needs and wants of others, you have no life energy left for your own needs and desires. An interesting fact about life is that, when you have satisfied your own emotional needs, you operate as a whole person with the emotional energy and insight to help others in need of support. Since you're not lugging around unnecessary emotional baggage such as insecurity, guilt, fear, doubts, and grudges, you're free to use your life energy more effectively. Learning to nurture yourself allows you to be more creative and resourceful in the challenges you face daily in this ever-changing world.

That you've chosen to open a book entitled *Feel and Grow Rich* suggests that some internal nudge is reminding you that you *do* have the power to have what you want in life. Perhaps you've forgotten your power to listen to the deepest part of yourself—your real needs, your desires, your gut instincts—and you've begun to make choices that are no longer satisfying. The good news is that your point of power is this minute in time. It's the decisions you will make and on which you will act from this day forward that will determine your destiny.

The purpose of this book is to give you the information, skills, and strategies that will assist you in empowering yourself to create whatever you want in life. You have within you all the talent and potential to manifest whatever you want. But there is a price tag. You must *feel* whatever you want inside of yourself, before you can manifest it into reality. You must *feel* rich to enjoy what blessings you already have to be able to create more. All success must be created internally before it can be created externally. This book can give you the motivation to use the talents already within you. You have the ability to tap into your own potential to create a wonderful, exciting, and wealthy life if you are open-minded and willing to try new strategies.

If we have learned anything from past decades, it is that success in life is measured by far more than money and titles and fancy material objects. What we really crave is a sense of fulfillment, which is more important than just "having it all." We want to fully experience what we have and what we can create. One of the most important by-products of getting in touch with your own needs and feelings is developing that ever-elusive "peace of mind." Developing the ability to have peace of mind is giving yourself permission to live your life free from fear, worry, guilt, and other negative feelings that drain you from living a "rich" life.

In the following pages, I'm going to share with you specific strategies and tools to help you recover a host of untapped resources and undiscovered options. You can take back your life and feel your own personal power to create whatever you want! But before we begin, let me state the ground rules up front: the past is a locked door; your future is made up of the choices you make today. Your power to live a life that fulfills you is determined by what actions you take today. You do not have to be a victim of past programming or past mistakes.

I don't buy the notion promoted by the media that life today is all "gloom and doom" and you don't have any power to change things—this is simply not true. In fact, I believe that life today holds unlimited possibilities for each of us to apply our talents in ways we may have never dreamed possible. What's more, if you do believe in the gloom-and-doom theory, you've got two strikes against you before you begin! Why? Because a lack of hope means that somewhere along the way you've stopped dreaming, and there's no way to make dreams come true, if you don't have any.

Life *has* changed, we are living in a new era. In the '80s we might have been willing to spend sixty to eighty hours per week in an unfulfilling job just to afford the big house, the fancy car and all the other trappings that go with the American Dream. In the '90s we're waking to the reality of just how much that "Dream" costs. With life as we know it changing more quickly than ever before and no guarantee for what the future will hold, many people are simply deciding to take back their lives. Collectively, we are realizing that simply working for material gain alone has not brought the fulfillment it once promised. Burned out and deeper in debt, we need to re-evaluate our lives and our future.

Our culture tends to perpetuate the myth that something or someone outside ourselves will make us happy. We tell ourselves: when I get that new car I'll be happy, when I get that new job, when I get that raise, when I have children. You do not have to have anything outside of yourself to become the person you want to be. You need to accept and feel the power you already have within you now.

I'm suggesting you take back your life and realize that you are the one with the power to make you happy or sad. You have the power to feel whatever you choose. The bottom line is that choice and not chance determines your future. The choices you make today will create your future. To really be in control in your life, you must become an actor in life and not a reactor to the circumstance. It's true that you may not have any control of outside events, but you do have the power within you to control your internal reactions.

As O.J. Simpson has said, "The day you take complete responsibility for yourself, the day you stop making excuses, that's the day you start to the top." Your power of choice is your one true personal power, and it is your greatest ally as you design your destiny. For it is your destiny you are ultimately shaping with the results of the choices you make every single day of your life. In fact, your power of choice is the only power you have that can ensure that you will create a life that fits your own unique personality and needs.

Anthony Robbins said in his book *Awaken the Giant Within*, "More than anything else, I believe it's our decisions, not the conditions of our lives, that determine our destiny." You must realize that you are responsible for the fulfillment of all your dreams. The power to succeed or fail is always yours to choose. No one can take this power away from you. You have the power to create whatever "riches" you want if you listen to yourself and feel what it is that you really want.

–2–
HOW TO ASK QUESTIONS
TO IMPROVE THE QUALITY OF YOUR LIFE

As a child growing up in rural Virginia—a mile from the nearest paved road off Chuckatuck Creek—I had none of the traditional advantages. Yet, despite the fact that I had no role models, no college degree, little money, and no connections for networking, I still beat all the odds. During those younger years, I spent a lot of time alone. In the evening after my parents and brother were asleep, I would tiptoe quietly outside, and, lying on the grass between our two German Shepherds, I would stare up at the sky for hours. Lying there hour after hour, listening to the horses graze lazily in the distance under the thousands of stars, I would dream about what life would be like when I grew up. How was it that some people seemed to become successful while others never found their dreams? What was the secret?

As I lay under the stars night after night, secretly pleased that no one knew I was there, I gradually became aware of a small voice inside. In fact, sometimes when I got really still, I would just *know* things. For one thing, I was certain I would never be happy living the life others expected of me. I wanted more. I wanted to see the world. I wanted to be independent. I wanted to feel in charge of my own destiny.

Today, in retrospect, I realize that one of my strongest assets was that I constantly asked questions—hundreds of them. And the singular question, "How do people manage to become successful?" beat like a drum through my days during those early years. You see, it baffled me how someone like myself—a naive country girl living eighteen miles from civilization, with little money, who wasn't particularly *good* in school and certainly didn't harbor any burning desire to go to college—could ever become successful. What's more, I was clueless about my talents—totally mystified about what I would do. But I never stopped asking questions, and eventually the questions led to my success.

I realize today that, if it hadn't been for my father, I probably wouldn't have realized the importance of what I'm about to share with you. You see, every night at sundown after the livestock had been fed and the chores were done, my family would sit around our big oak table, with the smell of fresh-baked bread and pipe tobacco filling the room, and my father would ask my brother and me what we had learned that day. Then he would present us with hypothetical situations and ask how we would handle them. Although at the time it seemed like a useless exercise, today I realize it actually helped infuse me with an "entrepreneurial" thinking process. I learned to tap into my own creative problem-solving talents and rely on my own gut instincts to overcome challenges. These exercises allowed me to develop a thinking process that would create the framework enabling me to become successful in making my dreams come true—a thinking process centered around asking questions and listening to my feelings.

The skills I developed from all those nights around the oak table has shown me a future brimming with opportunities for those having the courage to ask questions and seek new solutions. In fact, you now have the opportunity to create a life that is much more aligned with your own personal destiny—your deepest needs—a life that may well bring you far more satisfaction. So that's the good news. It's not that your "Dream" didn't come true; it's simply time to conjure up a new dream, to do a little soul-searching to become clear on exactly what you want. Not what your parents wanted, not the "Dream" that has been passed down from generation to generation, but your own unique future that you *can* dream into being. You begin that process by asking questions.

You see, asking questions is a critical process. By asking questions, you can outline all the available choices and determine a host of possible solutions. Then, you can receive valuable information you might not have thought of if you hadn't asked questions. The questions and answers will help you begin to develop strategies to take back your life.

In my lifelong search to discover the keys to success, I have spent years talking to people from across the country who have reached the top of their fields—people who systematically worked to make their dreams into realities. I noticed a trait common to all their lives; they asked questions—persistently. They didn't settle for what was on their plates. They wanted to know how it got there and why and what they could do to make it better. They questioned everything, and when the answers didn't come straight-away, they never got discouraged. They simply sought out others who had mastered similar challenges and asked for help.

In fact, I soon realized that these people had a different process for thinking than most. They were aware of the power of their minds and confident of their ability to eventually find an answer. These people were using their personal resources to question their hearts on what they really wanted. These successful people created not only wealth, but the quality of life that their hearts desired.

Today, I realize that effective thinking is actually the function of asking and answering questions. You see, in order to master your life, you must first master your thoughts. The brain is simply a sophisticated computer. When asked a question, it goes into "search mode" to find the answer. The subconscious mind is the data base from which a vast storehouse of answers is derived. And you can't access the data base until you "key in" the question. Then, your brain obediently offers up its information on anything you ask—just like a computer. The secret to success is to become aware of how to ask intelligent questions. Then you must listen to get the answers that will allow you to take positive steps toward achieving the results you want in your life.

There are several effective strategies that will enable you to tap into the power of your brain to receive the answers you need. First, it's important to develop an awareness of the type of questions you ask. For example, if you ask negative questions such as "Why am I stuck in this job?" or "Why can't I ever lose weight" or "Why is life so hard," you're focusing your thoughts on what is not working in your life. Accordingly, the answers your brain gives in response to negative questions will most likely be negative as well. For example, if you ask yourself why you're stuck in a dead-end job, your answer may be that no one is hiring new people or you are not smart enough to get something better. Then, you are simply left powerless—it's the old garbage-in-garbage-out theory.

What you must do is change your perception. You're not stuck or trapped by life. Your point of power is always in the present. The fact that you're reading this book means you have the desire to be in control of your destiny. You can create new options and new results by first asking questions that will focus your thinking on the vast data base of available choices and options stored in your mind. You see, everything you've ever experienced through your five senses is stored in your subconscious data base—all the experiences and every bit of knowledge you've ever been exposed to in your entire life is simply waiting for you to access it—all you have to do is ask the right questions.

In the beginning, you may have to ask yourself empowering questions several times before you train your thinking process to look for workable solutions: "What opportunities are available today that will help me become better and excel in my current situation?" or "What can I do to expand my scope and open the door to greater professional opportunities?" or "How can I have fun today and still accomplish everything I have to do?" Your brain will answer you with new options to consider.

You see, your thoughts create your emotions and, inevitably, your emotions direct your actions. If your problem is that you often get depressed and frustrated in your current situation and lose motivation, remember this: you can deal more effectively with your emotions by asking yourself questions that will change your focus. What you focus on, expands. When you focus on positives, you feel good; when you focus on negatives, you lose your power to act. If you make a mistake, don't ridicule yourself with *Why am I so stupid?* Why not ask what you can change so the same problem won't reoccur? Ask yourself what you can learn from the situation and how you can apply that knowledge to your benefit in the future. Questions are an important component of emotional management. And the quality of your questions determines the quality of your life. The bottom line is this: the best resource you have for success is to consistently focus on questions that will allow you to tap into your brain's resource bank to arrive at workable solutions. In truth, intelligent questions are the key to utilizing your power to create a happy, fulfilling life.

Now, you may be wondering what happens when, no matter how many questions you ask, you still don't get an answer? This is how learning to be aware of your gut instincts can be valuable. The thinking process I've been describing developed over years with daily exercise, training my brain to look for workable solutions. There were plenty of nights in the kitchen around the oak table when my father asked me a question about how to handle a situation that I couldn't answer, and he would simply say, "Relax and just give me your best guess." Often, the "guess" I would quickly blurt out would actually be the perfect solution. Now I realize he was teaching me to not only trust my inner feelings or instincts but also, when *I* asked a question and didn't get an answer, to ask again *persistently* and to *expect* to receive an answer—no matter what. This was a very important lesson. Today I've learned to use the same technique when up against any challenging situation. I ask myself, "What possible solution have I not thought of yet? What ways can I think about this situation that will lead me to an answer? What people or resources have I not tapped yet to arrive at a good, workable solution?"

I also learned that it wasn't just the questions I asked that were important, but the questions I failed to ask. For example, how would I respond if my particular choice didn't work? What then? Did I have another option? When was the last time you asked yourself critical questions such as "Am I happy? Is my life going in the direction I want? Are my present circumstances serving me?" If you're not asking these kinds of questions, how will you recognize that you need to make changes?

The questions you ask determine your focus in life. When we focus on what is negative—or what is not working—suddenly everything looks wrong, out-of-place, poorly timed. Our world seems out of synch. Here's an important thought for you: what if, instead of finding faults, problems, difficulties or always wishing your life could be different, you changed your focus? What if you accepted life for exactly what it is today and began to look for the "positives"—the advantages—and how you could make those positives even better? Focus on your blessings! Look at it this way: you have 1,440 minutes in each day to experience your life as joyful or miserable—it's your choice. For example, what if you were to see this particular time in history as positive. Think about it! With the "American Dream" in shambles, more and more people are disillusioned by the old structures that no longer seem to work. Now is the time to create new ways to live successfully in your own unique way. And in order to do so, empowering questions are more important than ever.

Begin by tossing out your old perceptions of what success used to mean and creating new ones. You do this by asking yourself what you want. What are you doing to create success for your future? In truth, learning to adapt to radically changed circumstances—like those of the '90s— gives us the opportunity to open new doors and create entirely new models for how to live. In fact, this new reality is forcing us, out of necessity, to question what our inner feelings are telling us about what we want in the future. While in the past we may have simply accepted the definition of success handed down from generation to generation, it does not make sense in today's world. Suddenly, people who never questioned life or the direction in which they were going find themselves analyzing everything.

Let me suggest daily exercises that will prompt you to ask yourself some very probing questions about your values and priorities. To make them more effective, invest in a journal or notebook to record your questions *and answers* on a daily basis. This is a powerful way to get answers from your subconscious mind. For example, write down your questions just before you go to sleep at night. When you awaken in the morning—before you read the newspaper or become involved in any activities—start writing as many answers to your questions as possible; the more answers, the better. Remember, all the information you need is already available in the data bank of your mind. You only have to access it by keying in a positive question.

Over a 21-day period, devote yourself to answering the following questions as truthfully as possible. You see, there have been a number of studies suggesting that it takes 21 days to create a habit. So, decide when you want to begin and be consistent. Answer the same questions everyday and try not to copy or duplicate the answers you wrote the day before. This process will help you to better understand what you want and help you to find creative new solutions to lingering old problems.

Beginning of the Day Exercise

Most people get up in the morning, go the bathroom mirror, look at themselves, and say things like *Why do I have to go to work today? Why am I out of shape?* The answers you get to negative questions like that don't make you feel motivated or excited about your upcoming day. Without realizing it, you have programmed yourself to feel out of control.

After your alarm goes off, stay in bed for a few extra minutes and begin asking yourself the following questions. Be sure to allow yourself time to find resourceful, positive answers. This will enable you to program your mind to see the positive aspects of your life—and ultimately enjoy it more.

1. What is positive or exciting about today?
2. What do I have to be grateful for?
3. How can I have fun today and still take care of my responsibilities?
4. How can I contribute more joy to my family and my business associates?
5. What am I willing to do to guarantee that I'll have fun today?

Try it. Notice that you gradually begin to feel more optimistic, energized, excited, and creative because you're looking for the good in your life; this is because you're not focusing on what you don't like. Actually, this exercise is an emotional management tool. The resourceful answers you get will help start your day off on a positive note. What you focus on becomes your reality. When you feel you're in control, you're more creative, have more fun, and experience far less stress. When you feel good about yourself, you're a better role model to your children, mate, and co-workers. *You* have the power to change your questions and, by doing so, change the quality of your life.

End of the Day Exercise

Then, before you go to sleep at night, answer the following questions:

1. What did I learn today that I didn't know before?
2. How can I use this information?
3. What good things happened today?
4. What can I do tomorrow to increase my abilities to make more money?
5. What actions do I need to take tomorrow to help me become more successful?
6. What happened today that, if I could, I would have done differently? What did I learn from the

experience? How can I make sure I won't make that mistake again?

Questions allow you to focus your attention and life energy on your talents and resources. The outcome is sure to be a better life.

–3–
HOW TO FIND YOUR TALENTS
AND CAPITALIZE ON THEM

I recommend you read the one-time best-seller *The Popcorn Report* by Faith Popcorn. This leading-edge marketer and trend-forecaster, whom *Fortune* magazine has called "the Nostradamus of Marketing," is predicting a consumer *revolt* that will affect every corporation and household in North America. The revolution will mean a massive change in what we buy and how we buy it and the quality of life we demand. Why? Because collectively, we have become disillusioned with corporations that have failed to deliver on their promises of security. We are disheartened with our banking systems which no longer seem as secure as in the past.

In the '90s, we are being forced to see life from an entirely different perspective. People are deciding to live more in the moment—since there are no more guarantees about what the future will hold, why not? Value has replaced image and intrinsic worth has replaced name brands. The trend now is to simplify and scale down. As a society, we are asking ourselves very important questions such as: What is really important? What is real? What is quality? The new reality of lack of security is forcing us to have the courage and flexibility to create in non-traditional ways. As a result, there will be new products to create, new markets to capture, and new trends that will impact your professional and personal lives—from your habits at work to your habits at play. The old standards are changing. Thousands of people will be changing jobs and launching new careers. It's up to you to recognize the opportunities, sense where the needs are, and create strategies to fill them. Your challenge is to use your skills and creative abilities in ways you may not have dreamed of before. It is up to you.

Did you get that, folks? That's great news. And if you're willing to be innovative and to take risks, anything is possible. Dr. Dennis Waitley, in his book *Winning the Innovation Game*, defined "innovators. . .as the trailblazers, the visionaries and the pioneers. Innovators have the visionary gift of looking ahead, the inventor's ability to create, and the entrepreneur's ability to sell. Above all, innovators have a burning desire to make their dreams into reality. They are not content to imagine the future; they want to create it."

So, if you think your chances of making your dreams come true are pretty slim, think again. New doors are opening today that will lead to opportunities, and these will allow you to apply your talents in ways you may never have imagined before. Remember that the old saying, "Necessity is the mother of invention," is true—particularly today. And the more talents you tap and skills you develop, the more leverage you will have in creating a happy, exciting, satisfying life style for yourself.

Creating a future in which you're using your natural talents—and feeling in charge of your life—is what this book is about. But perhaps you haven't discovered your true talents yet. If so, one of the most effective ways to tap into your potential and uncover your "uniqueness" is by looking at your past. In fact, if you look closely at the events that have led up to this moment, you may well discover a pattern in the history of your life—and hidden in that pattern is the key that will unlock your talents and enable you to become successful spending your time and life energy doing what you love.

You are the sum total of all your past choices. The good news is that you now can make new choices that will create a fulfilling successful future. Let me introduce to you a concept that I call the Time Line. The Time Line is a framework of the landscape of your life—a map of your direction and your choices. The Time Line will show you the critical turning points where you made important choices that would eventually determine your skills and talents. By taking a closer look at this "roadmap," you will see options for the future.

You will see that your life has been a step-by-step preparation for what you would do next. What's more, you will recognize that every experience you have ever had until now has simply been an important learning experience. And once you see where you've been, you'll have more information to see where you're going. It's important to realize that you are not a reactor to life or circumstances; you have the power to make choices and chart the course of your life. If you acknowledge the lessons, skills, and experiences you already have, then you will have more resources to decide where you want to focus your life energy in the future.

Although we have been exposed to thousands of valuable learning experiences throughout our lives, much of this learning has simply been locked away in our subconscious, waiting to be accessed. By outlining your childhood experiences, your most positive work experiences, and your dreams and visions, you will establish a foundation of meaning for how you got where you are today in your conscious mind. Then, your reasons for living up to this point will be behind you and pushing you forward. The Time Line will act as a beacon that will light the way to your future. Without this foundation of self-knowledge, you could spend your entire life confused about your direction. It's important to eliminate confusion on your life's direction, once and for all.

Let me give you an example of how I used the Time Line to discover my own unique talents. And, most importantly, how to capitalize on these talents. By mapping out my own past, I was able to clearly see the critical turning points that became the pathway taking me to where I am today and where my options will be in the future.

When I was younger, I spent a great deal of time alone, riding my horse through the miles of open fields surrounding my parents' farm. While I rode, I would daydream and imagine myself grown up. In my mind's eye, I would see myself standing on a stage before thousands of people, a microphone clutched in my hand. Since a stage and a microphone meant "singer" to me, I figured I'd eventually become a singer. Other times, I would imagine I was a famous writer. I'd stay up till all hours of the night, telling stories that would help people live a better life.

Eventually, after entering junior high and realizing that I had no musical talent whatsoever and the ability to write clearly escaped me, I began searching for the key that would somehow unlock the door to my success. I knew I wanted to be successful, but what could I do to get there? What were my talents? In retrospect, I clearly see an event that occurred in the seventh grade that could have shaped and guided my search to discover my talents. Unfortunately, I didn't know enough to pay attention to the signpost!

I remember it as if it were yesterday because it was the first time in my life that I had ever excelled at anything while in school. My teacher, Mrs. Lane, had given us an assignment: each of us was to deliver a five-minute speech to the class on the subject of our choice. There was only one thing I wanted to talk about—my passion, horses. I lived and breathed horses. In fact, my mother used to kid me that my room always smelled like saddles. And it did, simply because I would drag my saddle upstairs into my room weekly to clean and polish it. And every wall was covered with pictures and posters of every imaginable breed of horse, from thoroughbreds to quarter horses.

But when the day came to give my speech and share my excitement with the other students, I was as nervous as all the other students in that lime-green-trailer-turned-into-a-classroom. I had never stood in front of a group before, much less given a speech. When it was my turn, I walked to the front of the classroom and, despite my sheer terror, launched into a discussion about the history of horses. Suddenly, something shifted inside me. I forgot all about my notes and became so immersed in sharing my knowledge and excitement that I talked well over the allotted time. When I finished, I looked over at Mrs. Lane staring at me with a surprised look; she blurted out, "Oh, my God. You can actually do something well!"

Three years after my experience in Mrs. Lane's seventh-grade class, another experience demonstrated an inner talent. In tenth grade, I won a competition for public speaking and eventually placed in the finals for the entire school. Yet once again, it never occurred to me that I had a talent upon which I could eventually capitalize to make my dream of success come true.

By the time I was seventeen and midway through my senior year of high school, I was in a panic. Most of my classmates already knew what they were going to do when they graduated. But I remained lost and spent hours in the guidance counselor's office asking question upon question to somehow uncover what I might do in the future. My parents had made it clear that college was out of the question. There was simply no money. And although I had been working by then for many years in part-time jobs after school, I certainly didn't have enough money to afford tuition, even for the nearest community college. I wanted to live on my own and work; I just had no idea where or how.

Then, one day in February, opportunity knocked. I heard about a radio station in the city of Norfolk, eighteen miles away, that was looking to hire a disc jockey for the weekend shift. Although I told them a "white lie"—that I was nineteen and just out of school—they hired me on the spot. I was dumbstruck! Finally, I'd found something that might take me from the confusion I had been feeling—a direction in which to move.

That event was a turning point for me, a critical opportunity that would help to open a series of doors in the upcoming years. Working as a disc jockey forced me out of my shyness and enabled me to foster a more outgoing personality. I developed confidence and, more importantly, an awareness of my ability to communicate well. In short, I learned to have fun and get paid for it! In fact, during that time, working on weekends and attending school during the week, I was awakened to an entirely new world filled with people with very different values and goals than the ones I'd known before.

An added benefit was that I realized that my co-workers had come to be successful in a variety of different ways. As I got to know them better and listened to each of their stories, I suddenly realized that there wasn't just one road to success—there were many. After getting to know these people, I realized that they didn't have anything I didn't have. So, I figured if they could do it, so could I.

Four months later, after graduation, Lady Luck arrived once again when I was offered a full-time position selling advertising time. Suddenly, I'd found my niche—I was a natural at sales. In fact, it led me to where I am today. That experience of dealing with hundreds of different people from all walks of life, each with their unique problems, was a training ground. It taught me to deal with people when I became a professional speaker and business woman owning my own company ten years later. It was one of the critical turning points on my Time Line.

If I hadn't gone into sales, I might never have developed the skills needed to be a speaker and author. What's more, it gave me my first real taste of being self-employed. I was forced to become highly organized and very self-motivated. And in recognizing that each person was different, I learned how to customize my message to that person's needs. If one approach was not effective, I learned to shift my focus and find new ways to communicate the same information in a way that was understood. I will always be grateful for that opportunity simply because it gave me the framework to build and shape my career.

I did the Time Line, for the first time, during a period in my career when I felt as if I had reached a dead end. I wanted to enjoy my work again, yet I wasn't clear about the direction I could take. All along, my dearest friends continued to tell me that I had the personality, talent, and drive to start my own training company and be a professional speaker. My initial reaction was that it was impossible since I had no training in this area. Eventually, I developed an attitude that gave me the courage to take a leap of faith. It was up to me to go for what I wanted in life and the only limits were those I created with my thoughts.

In truth, this attitude is the essence of what success is about. You have the power to do *whatever* you want; the first step to success is desire. By utilizing your own Time Line, you too can reawaken your desires and see new possibilities. In fact, as a result of many of the changes we are experiencing in today's world, there is more opportunity than ever before to make your dreams into reality.

If you already feel you've found your niche in life and have no desire to change direction at this time, simply read the exercises and move on to the next chapter. If you don't know what you want to be when you grow up or if your life seems uncertain, the following exercise will change your view of your possibilities. I am the first to admit that undertaking this exercise will take time, effort, and courage. But the payoff will be finding options on how to earn a living doing what you really love. Most people expect some neon sign in the sky telling them what to do with their lives or how to earn a living; you may have noticed it doesn't happen like that. You have the opportunity with this exercise to open new doors and truly find your power to live a rich life doing what you want.

How to Create Your Own Time Line

To create your own Time Line, relax and pay attention to whatever memories come drifting into your mind in response to the questions in the following pages. And remember: do not edit your past or stop yourself from remembering some event because you think you could never use that skill in the future. Just allow yourself to remember times in your past when you really enjoyed yourself—whether at work or at play—and the times you surprised yourself by doing something exceptionally well.

The Time Line consists of three parts—the CHILDHOOD AND ADOLESCENCE Time Line, the VISION/DREAM Time Line and the WORK Time Line. After you've mapped out these three areas, you will be able observe many of your skills, desires, and natural abilities, and certain traits about yourself that are signals of hidden talent. These abilities can give you options to capitalize on to make money and do what you enjoy in your life.

Now that you have an idea of what can be accomplished by using the Time Line, here are the "nuts and bolts" of how to begin:

1. Buy a journal or notebook specifically for the Time Line exercises.

2. Divide it into three sections. One section for Childhood and Adolescence, one for your Vision/Dream Time Line, and one for your Work Time Line. Give yourself plenty of space to go back and fill in thoughts that may come to you later. Then, establish a particular hour of the day when you will be undisturbed for at least ten to fifteen minutes. I suggest you try this first thing in the morning while you're fresh, or just before going to sleep at night. Turn off the phone; and, if other people live in the house, let them know that you wish to be alone. Then create an enjoyable, soothing environment. For example, you may want to wear loose clothing, as it is important to feel comfortable and relaxed. Then, close your eyes and begin breathing slowly and let all your concerns fade away. You may even want to put on some gentle, calming music to help you drift back gently into the memories of your past.

3. When you begin, write your questions in your journal, then write your answers. Again, do not edit—just allow your thoughts to flow on paper.

4. Once you start this process, the answers will begin to come at various times during the day, so it's important to carry a small notebook with you to jot down any passing thoughts. We all have good intentions to remember the revelation when we get home, but in reality it's easy to

forget. Don't let those gems of thought get away!

5. One of the most effective ways to map out your Time Line is to give yourself 21 days to do the exercise. Ask the same questions over and over and watch the most resourceful answers pile up. The advantage of playing with this exercise every day at the same time is that it allows your brain to create a habit pattern. And since the brain loves consistency, it will automatically begin coming up with answers at that time every day.

Begin the process with the Childhood and Adolescence Time Line. Visualize yourself as a child. Allow yourself to feel as you felt then. Remember what games you used to play—your favorite places to hide. Allow the good memories to come back, so you can notice your choices.

Divide your life into critical time periods, i.e., childhood, adolescent years. Then, ask yourself the following questions.

Childhood, Adolescence "Time Line"

What was your very first memory?

What was the first thing you can remember that you did extremely well?

Did other people notice and compliment you on your ability?

What were your dreams?

What did you want to be when you grew up?

Who did you admire?

What subjects did you like in school?

What did other people—family members, teachers or friends—tell you that you would be good at when you grew up?

What subjects did you really enjoy learning in school?   What extracurricular activities did you really enjoy?

What subjects did you learn most easily?

Whatever you discover about your past, keep a record of it in your journal. Don't think you will remember; it's important to write these memories down. (I promise it will pay off later.) Then, try to isolate events or signals that would indicate some natural talent, as I shared with you on my own Time Line about my seventh-grade experience.

The formula I used to find my talents was deciding to have fun doing this project. I enjoyed my trip down memory lane by first going through my memorabilia, interviewing my family and childhood friends, and then writing what I discovered in my journal. I wrote down whatever I could remember from each grade and each stage in life. I treated the project as if it were my biography.

It's okay if you don't remember very much; the objective is to look for signs of talent or skills that you can use now. It doesn't require a lot of time, about ten minutes a day. I personally found this exercise to be very rewarding because it allowed me to remember things I had not thought of in many years. It also allowed me to appreciate where I had been and where I am today. I acknowledged my struggles, my victories, and my learning.

Keys to your natural talents may also be found in your dreams and visions about the ideal life. Dreams show you your potential and direct you to things you can accomplish. Do not discard your dreams and visions as silly, impractical, or childish illusions. Honor them as messages from your deepest inner wisdom, showing you that you *do* have talents and gifts.

Answer the following questions for your Vision/Dream Time Line:

When you were a child, what were your fantasies and dreams?

Who were your heroes?

Who did you admire and what was it about these people that you admired?

Name your favorite books or movies that you wanted to see again and again.

Do you have any dreams today that may be signals of how you might use your talents in ways you have not used them before?

What are your secret desires? If money were not an issue, what would you do with your life and time?

Work Time Line:

Every job you have ever had, every skill you ever learned is a stepping stone to your future. You will see this after you finish. In your journal, use one page for every job you've ever had. Write the job at the top of each page. Then, answer the following questions on each page. When you've finished answering each question, write a short summary of the jobs that you enjoyed the most.

What activities in each of the jobs did you most look forward to accomplishing?

What activities in each job gave you the most pleasure? What activities brought you the most compliments?

What were the positives in each situation?

How did each job experience educate and prepare you for your next job?

Everything you enjoy doing—every job, activity or hobby—involves the use of certain skills. You must now ask yourself the following questions:

What are your hobbies?

What voluntary activities do you do simply because you enjoy them? What activities make you feel energized and alive?

Are you more interested in people skills, working with your hands, or technical skills?

Are you attracted to business skills, negotiating, managing, leading, organizing, networking?

Are you attracted to scientific or research skills?

Does writing or counseling interest you?

Do you like to work with computers and mechanical equipment?

Are you interested in statistics or numbers?

Do you enjoy working with your imagination and creativity?

Are you attracted to the arts, singing or dancing?

Are you more comfortable in logical, analytical work?

What type of work would you do, even without pay, simply because you enjoy it?

After completing all three of the Time Lines, you will see how your life has been a preparation for every step you've ever taken. You needed all those unique experiences, skills, and knowledge to progress to more challenging opportunities. You should notice now how your life has prepared you for what you will do in the future. Look at the Time Line as a ladder; each job leads to new opportunities for the future. The choices you made determined the path you moved along to get where you are today.

Naturally, once you have identified your skills, you can concentrate on developing practical strategies to use your talents in your daily life to earn money. The Time Line will help you become aware of the rich and varied background of skills and abilities you have within you. The more detail and clarity you bring to your Time Line, the more you will be able to see opportunities you've never identified before. What's more, you will be able to see if you work more effectively in a structured career, such as working for a large corporation, or if you are the kind of person that works best in a job that offers freedom and autonomy such as sales or self-employment.

Now, before you begin to trace out your hidden talents, congratulate yourself on doing a great job by recording your history. Then, you will need to take all the information and look for options. The way I summed up my options was to use a large poster board and create at least five columns. Answer the following questions from the information written in your journal.

In column one, list all the work-related experiences you truly enjoyed. For example, you love working with people and you enjoy freedom and creativity. In column two, list your work experiences such as sales clerk, teacher, etc. In column three, list your strongest personal traits; for example, you are a good communicator or you are a team player. In column four, list your business strengths, such as you are a good manager or you are an excellent typist or mechanic. In column five, list what *you* consider to be your business weaknesses. Perhaps you don't like working with machines, or you're not good in math, or you prefer to work alone. Add as many columns as you like. Try to get a picture of who you are onto the poster board.

Now, here comes the fun part; it's time to brainstorm! Act as if the person whose history is on that poster board *is* a stranger. Ask what options this person has to creatively use their talents; don't limit your thinking—write down all possible options. For example, when I did my first Time Line and summarized my findings, I came up with career options I had not considered before. You too will find lots of options you may have never considered before.

I strongly suggest you do the following exercise with some of your most supportive friends or family members. According to Napoleon Hill, author of *Think and Grow Rich*, "Brains are like batteries. The more batteries you have, the more power you have." So, the more people—i.e., brains—you have working together for a harmonious purpose, the more creative information you will come up with. But remember, it's important to share this process only with people who are supportive.

Once you have gathered all this information, *ask* yourself, "What am I going to do with it?"

CHAPTER
_4_
SUCCESS SELF-PROGRAMMING

How to Motivate Yourself

Learning the art of self-motivation is one of the most powerful and rewarding gifts you can give yourself. Until now, you may have depended on others to motivate you, but the truth is—all motivation comes from within. In fact, the difference between a successful person and an average person *is* their degree of motivation.

One of the first steps toward developing self-motivation is to create desire. Napoleon Hill, author of the most popular success books in our time, *Think and Grow Rich* and *Laws of Success*, said, "The starting point of all achievement is desire. Keep this constantly in mind. Weak desire brings weak results, just as a small amount of fire makes a small amount of heat."

The purpose of the Time Line exercise in Chapter 3 was to awaken your deepest, most passionate desires and tap into your true talents. Think about it. In order to use your life energy in the most effective way, you must tap into your deepest motivation, your desires. By the time you completed each of your Time Lines, you probably began to see some of the secret or hidden dreams you've long desired—but have been afraid to admit. And when your desire strengthens, your motivation increases ten-fold. Your desires are a critical factor in what you accomplish in life. Most of us have been taught to not honor our deepest desires, but to follow more traditional safe paths.

Not too long ago I took my next door neighbor, eighty-eight-year-old Mrs. Holly, out to dinner. In the midst of our conversation, she said, "It's never your mistakes that eat you alive—it's the missed opportunities. Mistakes are simply chances to try again, but missed opportunities are lost forever and remain to haunt you." As a young woman in the early 1930s, Mrs. Holly had a passionate desire to become an artist, but no one in her family believed she had talent. Eventually she gave up her heart's desire and became a housewife like most women of her day. Today, she still gets teary-eyed when she talks about it. What's more, she said, if she were young again, nothing on earth could stop her from going abroad and becoming an artist. As Pearl Buck said, "There were many ways of breaking a heart. . . but what really broke a heart was taking away its dream—whatever that dream might be."

The truth for many of us is that the passionate desire to live out our dreams has been forgotten. All too often, we have put them on a shelf to care for other's needs and desires. We are the cheerleaders and supporters of others, yet we haven't given ourselves permission to go for our own dreams and desires. Don't let yourself be another Mrs. Holly, in the twilight of your life with memories of what you wanted to do but didn't because of circumstances. Life is too short to not look honestly at yourself and ask, "What do I want? What desires do I have that I have not yet fulfilled?" What can you do today to really live your life, not just exist?

You need to listen to the inner you, reawaken your deepest desires and begin to take specific action toward fulfilling them—no matter how long it takes. Remember, destiny is not a matter of chance—it's a matter of choice. Your power to be rich starts with the desire to use your talents, skills, and abilities in ways that make you happy. I love the old saying "Success is not a still picture, it's a moving picture." It says to me that success is the way you live your life; it's what you do every day that counts.

Another important key to developing a strong sense of self-motivation is to examine your beliefs—both about your-self and about what is possible. Belief in yourself is the starting point for all achievement. It takes a lot of courage to dare to make your dreams come true, and belief in yourself is the one basic, absolutely essential ingredient for anyone who wants to begin. What's more, it's the powerful driving force behind all great success. You choose what you will believe every day—both about yourself and what you can accomplish—and this simple analysis determines who you are and who you will become more than any other factor.

When I take a close look at my life, I realize I could never have gone for my dreams without a strong belief in myself *and* a belief that I could do what other people said was impossible. Let me give you an example. At the age of twenty-eight, after a number of sales positions and one year into my career as a commercial real estate agent, I woke up one morning and simply did not want to get out of bed. The cold truth hit me in the face—I hated my job. I had lost my motivation. Life was no longer fun. In fact, after a little soul-searching, I had to admit to myself that I'd only gone into real estate chasing the lure of big bucks. And unfortunately, not only was I not making the big bucks, but my life was filled with frustration. What was occurring—although I didn't realize it at the time—was that my belief systems were changing. I had stopped believing that real estate was the career for me. What's more, my beliefs about success were changing. Up to that point, I had been moving through life determined to establish a life style that I believed meant success—money, titles, and lots of fancy trappings. Clearly, I was at a critical point in my life. I could sell out and continue working in a job that did not bring me happiness, or I could begin to reevaluate and restructure my beliefs about what was really important. Money, or happiness? Why couldn't I have both?

Even with the pain and confusion I was feeling at that moment, I could still hear the small voice inside—the same voice that had, since the beginning, led me through the darkest of moments—telling me to pay attention and look at what in my life was not working. Then I would have to simply take the time to get clear on my new beliefs and allow them to motivate me toward my next level of success. So, after many tears and lots of long sleepless nights, I finally began to ask myself some of the most important questions of my life. What did I love to do most? How did I want to live each day? What could I do that would allow me to wake up each morning excited about the day ahead? How could I earn a living and love what I do?

Looking back, I realize it took a great deal of courage to face the reality that my life was not working and attempt to do something about it. I was twenty-eight years old, hadn't finished college, and had no intention of returning to school. What's more, I knew in my heart that, whatever I decided from that point forward, I would *have* to be independent. I had paid my dues making other people money. I was ready to do something that really excited and fulfilled me. I was ready to start my own business. I was ready to launch a new dream—this time, one that was closer to the "real me."

A few weeks later, after a great deal of soul-searching, I created an opportunity at the real estate firm where I was working. The owners had been so wrapped up in their day-to-day problems that they were not training their employees to deal with the problems of the future. So, I proposed conducting a pilot training program that would empower their people to deal more effectively with the changes that were occurring due to the recession. To my surprise, they loved the idea and I set to work immediately! For the next three months, I worked nearly fourteen hours a day, researching and writing the program. The time went quickly because I enjoyed learning so much new information. On the big day, though ready to present the training program that I had written, I was terrified. Yet, after I began speaking, I felt as if I had been doing it my entire life. I was thrilled to have the opportunity to inspire people to make profound changes in their lives. In fact, I was so certain that this was what I wanted to do with my life that I took a leap of faith. Within a week, after the program was complete, I resigned from the firm to start my own training company—once again with the firm belief that I *must* go for my dreams.

However, within a few weeks, the cold, hard reality of my impulsive move hit me in the face. Suddenly I realized that I was clueless as to how to earn a living as a professional speaker. I had leaped before I had looked and now was forced to trust and believe the prompting of an inner voice that, so far, had never steered me wrong. With no other choice—since I wasn't willing to give up yet—I once again set to work and painstakingly attempted to come up with a plan. After all, I *did* know how to sell myself and how to market products. And I was blessed with good common sense about what worked in business. Over the next three years, I paid the bills—but I nearly starved. And I'll be honest, I was scared. I had sold nearly everything of value just to get by—my home, my stocks and my beloved jewelry. The only thing that kept me going was the total, absolute belief that somehow I could make this business work.

Today, I know that people who dare to believe in themselves are willing to take more risks. And the more attempts you make toward making your dreams come true, the more chance you have of achieving success. You see, there is nothing mystical or magical about the power of belief. It simply works; when you have the can-do attitude, it gives the brain the power, skill, and energy needed to accomplish whatever challenge you give it. The "how-to-do-it" always comes to the person who believes "they-can-do-it." Once again, it's simply the power of belief. Strong beliefs trigger the mind to figure out the details of how to succeed; it's how ideas are born. And without the driving force of belief in yourself, you won't have the courage, interest, or enthusiasm to keep going when times get rough.

In the words of the famous Irish poet George Russell, "We become what we contemplate." We are self-fulfilling prophecies. It doesn't matter if your beliefs are true or false; your beliefs eventually become facts. Whatever beliefs you have formed about yourself are exactly what you will act on. For example, when you have the attitude, "I'll give this project a try but I don't think it will work," you've failed before you've begun! When your mind doubts your ability, it is attracted to events to support the belief that you're not capable of succeeding; and then you fail. It's that simple.

It may help you to think of it this way. Your belief systems are like a thermostat; they regulate what you accomplish in life. When you don't believe you're worth much, you don't ask for much. When you think you're unable to do great things, you won't try to achieve great things. If you think you're stuck, you become stuck because you don't believe you have the power to change your circumstances for the better. You must have a strong, firm belief in yourself first, or your desires will never have a chance to manifest.

No matter how great your ability, how large your genius, or how extensive your education, your achievement will never rise higher than the confidence you have in yourself. In the words of the late Henry Ford, "If you think you can or if you think you cannot, you are always right." This is an indisputable law of life. Whatever you believe about yourself will determine how much time you devote to making your dreams come true and the skills and knowledge you will inevitably use. Many people go through life thinking that other people's successes are out of their reach—that the rewards of life go only to the special people. They don't realize how they sabotage themselves by this attitude of self-deprecation or self-effacement. They accept only what is given to them in life and expect very little. Giving yourself permission to believe in yourself is one of the greatest gifts you have. And the more you believe in yourself, the more you expect of your life—and "life" delivers!

Remember, you don't have to live a mediocre life; you don't have to be average; you don't have to let your past keep you from creating a wonderful, exciting future. You can start today to appreciate yourself and be the master of your own destiny by being willing to believe in your own unique abilities. There is an old proverb, "If there is no wind, row!" It is very empowering to realize that, by choosing our beliefs about our circumstances, we can powerfully affect the outcome. Don't get me wrong—I'm not suggesting that changing beliefs and becoming successful is simple; it also takes a great deal of hard work.

In that first three years, while trying to earn a living as a professional speaker, I did everything I could to be successful and change my beliefs about what I could accomplish. I marketed my training courses to local businesses, I taught non-accredited sales courses for the local college, and I promoted real estate seminars. But for the most part, I ended up speaking to clubs and organizations for free—if only for the experience and exposure. What's more, I did not sit idly in my office waiting for the phone to ring. When I was not actively marketing, I was educating myself. I attended every seminar I could find on speaking. I studied how other speakers used humor, how they organized material, how they grabbed the attention of an audience. I even interviewed them about their beliefs and strategies and how they stayed motivated during tough times. I had to know everything about these people—from the books they read, to how they spent their spare time. And most importantly, I did everything possible to keep *myself* motivated.

I listened to motivational tapes every chance I had, while getting dressed for the day, or working around the house, or cutting the grass, or driving. Every spare moment, I saturated my mind with all the positive, motivational, and educational material I could find. I realized that my fate was in my own hands. There was no one to blame but myself if I didn't give this career everything I had. I promised myself that I would do whatever it took for five years, and if this new business was not successful, I would then turn my energy into another direction. With that commitment made, I did everything that other successful people did to become successful; I focused all my life energy into my goal and did whatever it took.

What's more, I surrounded myself with positive people who were also excited about my goals. People who were supportive and helpful and were there for me when I was feeling down and scared. I had to make sure I was nurturing my mind and spirit as much as possible. It would have been so easy to fall off the wagon and see the reality facing me as nearly impossible. There were days I could have easily given up—when the phone didn't ring and money was low. But the one thing that kept me going was that I continued to believe in myself. I kept affirming, "I can do this, I can become successful." My energy was focused on what my life would be like when I became an accomplished speaker. I clung to the belief that I had what it took to become successful in my field—even when there was no physical evidence that I would make it.

Perhaps it's destiny or just the result of a lot of hard work, but just when I thought I had been totally wrong to believe I had what it took to succeed in my chosen field, just when I felt I'd done everything I knew and nothing worked, I got my first break. I was hired to speak at a regional sales meeting on personal motivation. And, this one big break (thankfully!) opened the door to my career as a professional speaker and helped seal my fate.

Today I know I could never have endured until that opportunity came along if I hadn't continued to bolster my beliefs with a host of techniques to keep me motivated. You can do the same. Why not start today to feed your mind with information that is uplifting? Begin reading biographies of successful people and expose yourself to the trials and challenges these people experienced. Then, you will not feel so alone in your search for success. Reading the stories of other people's lives has always given me great insight on how to handle problems and situations. In fact, I honestly believe that I have saved myself countless mistakes by learning from the experience of others. I simply molded and shaped their strategies into my own personality and career. As Woodrow Wilson once said, "I not only use all the brains I have but all the brains I can borrow from others."

Control Your Thoughts

Another critical key to developing self-motivation is to control your thoughts. This is certainly not new information; it has been taught for centuries by many of the world's most famous teachers. Buddha said, "All that we are is the result of what we have thought." Ralph Waldo Emerson declared that "The ancestor of every action is thought." As Napoleon Hill said, "You have absolute control over but one thing—your thoughts. This divine prerogative is the sole means by which you may control your destiny. If you fail to control your mind, you will control nothing else. Your mind is your spiritual estate. What you hold in your mind today will shape your experiences of tomorrow."

To take charge of your destiny, you must take charge of your thoughts. The first step is to become aware that your brain is a very sophisticated computer; we are made of more than just flesh and blood. In fact, we literally have four volts of electricity in our body. And every time we have a thought—good or bad, right or wrong, true or false—that four volts of electricity goes from the conscious mind into the subconscious mind and creates a sort of "groove." That groove translates into a picture; human beings think in pictures and the objective of the subconscious mind is to match the pictures in your mind with the reality that manifests in your daily life. So—all success must be created in the mind before you can create it in reality.

Self-Image

Even more important is the fact that your self-image is formed by your daily thoughts, and your self-image is the core of your being. It determines everything about you—how you will take risks, how much you will believe in yourself, and how motivated you are. In fact, your self-image determines your eventual success in every way—how you keep your personal appearance, how much money you make, how many calculated risks you take, how you will nurture yourself, the success of your relationships, how good you are at sports. Everything is determined by your self-image. Psychologists tell us that, in the first five to seven years of life, our self-image is formed by our parents, peers, teachers, and society. Much of that original picture of yourself will persist and influences how successful you are today. If, as children, you were exposed to negative information about yourself, those negative opinions may be impacting your abilities and potential today.

When you consider the brain as a computer, you can act only in a manner that will match the pictures of who you think you are and what you think you can do. Sometimes limiting pictures have been programmed in our brain, holding you back from reaching your true potential. The great news is that you have the power today to reprogram yourself with new empowering information. You're not stuck with old programs. If you've told yourself negative things about yourself, or other people have told you negative things, then start today to reprogram positive messages with your thoughts and self-talk. Just as you cannot harvest oranges from apple trees, you cannot think thoughts of lack and reap success and prosperity. Your subconscious mind is your slave. All thoughts, fears, and emotions send pictures from the conscious mind through the nervous system to the subconscious, and the body prepares to act on the request. The subconscious, like the earth, simply reproduces what is planted in it. If you have unhealthy emotions of imagined fears, worry, resentment, or guilt, the body responds with a tense feeling of nervousness, stress-related illness, tiredness, and lack of energy and creativity. Your subconscious mind will produce whatever you ask for. As a powerful computer, it doesn't care what information you put in, it simply acts on all information as if it were true. Shakespeare once said, "There is nothing good or bad, but thinking has made it so."

You were not born with negative information about yourself. Any limiting information in your brain came from outside sources. You cannot fully utilize your potential until you decide to take responsibility for the caliber of information you put into your mind.

Programming Yourself for Success

A very easy way for you to begin using your power to create the future you want is to simply think of your mind as your personal computer. It has two distinct parts that are under your control: the conscious mind, the part of your mind that is rational, knows right from wrong, directs your thoughts and makes decisions; and the subconscious mind, a huge memory bank that records everything that you have ever heard, read, seen, or told yourself. Your subconscious records every thought that goes through your conscious mind through all of the five senses. These thoughts are then classified and recorded so they can be recalled through memory.

Your subconscious mind doesn't know right from wrong. It simply receives and files the thoughts; it does exactly what the conscious mind tells it to do. According to scientists, your subconscious mind will hold more information than all the libraries in the entire world put together. Your power to be whatever you want starts with the desire and commitment to program new information into your computer, information that makes you feel good about yourself and allows you to use your potential. New beliefs created from your new thoughts will enable you to stay motivated to do whatever it takes to reach your goals or dreams.

As the most important organ in the body and a highly sophisticated memory bank, the mind works upon the information and data you feed into it every day and creates the reality of your life. That's why it's so important to carefully consider the kind of information you feed your mind. Everything that you think—true or false, good or bad—goes from the conscious mind and imprints on the subconscious. That information is translated into a picture. So, whatever information is programmed into your subconscious about your abilities, your potential and your worth is what you believe to be true and becomes your self-image. Too often, you don't see your real talents and skills; you simply see the information that has been programmed into your computer from outside sources and your outdated thoughts. And your self-image—whether real or illusionary—is a foundation upon which your entire future is built. You will simply act out the type of person you conceive yourself to be, based upon your own beliefs about yourself.

It's no wonder that some of us fail at new ventures before we even start. Unless we take charge of the caliber of information that goes into our computer and change our inner pictures, we will be saddled with an outdated self-image and a comfort zone that will not allow us to become motivated to make our dreams come true. In the words of Dr. Maxwell Maltz, in his famous book *Psycho-Cybernetics*, "The self-image sets the boundaries of individual accomplishment. It defines what you can and cannot do. Expand the self-image and you expand the areas of the possible." The development of a positive, realistic self-image will imbue your life with new capabilities and new talents and literally turn a life of constant failure into one of repeated success. Decide today to no longer be a victim of the past. Consciously decide to change old negative programs and give yourself a new lease on life. You can do that by maintaining constant awareness about your daily thoughts.

You've heard the old saying that people teach what they most need to learn. This has been particularly true in my life. As a child, I had a very poor self-image. Although my "inner voice" kept affirming that I had something important to offer to the world, my environment did nothing to reinforce it. It wasn't until I decided to take charge of my destiny and change my life that I really started seeking help. I read every book I could find on self-image and personal empowerment and gradually, over the years, gained the courage and resources to revamp the negative picture of myself. Today, I know that this was one of the most critical decisions in my life. Without changing my self-image, I could never have created a better life for myself doing what I really love to do. I would have simply continued living without using my inborn talents and most likely would have ended up an unfulfilled person.

Personal Power

Often, as I travel around the country, I hear many people blaming the past for their lack of a happy present life. I hear things like: it's my parents' fault, something bad happened to me, or I don't know how to change. The reality of life is that we have all had challenges and obstacles to overcome, but we cannot blame the past for our current behavior and decisions. If you look at the past, you will see that your parents were doing the best they could at the time with the knowledge and resources they had available. They were not exposed to the self-help material to which we have access today. They were simply victims of victims. They were raised by their parents who may have had some limiting belief systems. But today, we *do* have the tools to break the cycle of the past and take 100-percent responsibility for our beliefs and motivation and stop blaming the past. You must remember that you create your own reality with your thoughts. And feeling energized and excited about a desire or dream is what will keep you feeling alive and excited about your future. This is the essence of personal power, the path to self-motivation.

Victory Book

One of the tools I used to help me stay motivated, to go for my dreams, and to overcome the old programming from the past was the "Victory Book." Let me explain. I simply purchased a large, inexpensive photo album and filled it with all my past successes—pictures, awards, articles about myself, letters of congratulation. This book was not a "brag book" to show other people; it was a tool—only for myself—that I used to remind myself just how far I'd come. Eventually, it became a ritual: every morning before I began working, I would sit at my desk and go through my Victory Book to reinforce my beliefs that I had the talent, skill, knowledge, and persistence to succeed. No matter what challenges came my way, I had the resources to handle it—after all, the evidence was before me! What I was really doing was programming my mind to have confidence. I was also using the Victory Book as a tool to feel in control and powerful in my life.

Even today, when I have a bad day or I have made a mistake or failed at something, I still take the time to go back over my Victory Books of the past. I have them lined up in my personal office, so that anytime I need a boost, I can easily pull them out and acknowledge my hard work, my devotion, and my tenacity. There is nothing that can give you more motivation than acknowledging the success you've already enjoyed. I would like to suggest to parents that you start a Victory Book for each of your children. Every time they get good report cards or do things that they are proud of, please put them in their books. The next time your children come home fearful about not being able to do something, pull out the Victory Books and remind them how they were successful in the past. This one tool will build self-confidence for your children. (Wouldn't it have been great if you had a Victory Book growing up?)

–5–
YOUR DECLARATION OF INDEPENDENCE

When I was in the fourth grade, I was a very average student. My favorite classes were art and recess. I remember being very nervous coming home from school one day because I had gotten an "F" in Spelling on my report card. I knew my parents would be very upset that I had failed and would expect me to study more and put me on house restriction.

So I did what every normal child would do and tried to make up for the bad grade by doing some good things right away. I went home and cleaned my room, I volunteered to help with dinner, I emptied the trash, and I was even nice to my little brother. However, my mother is not stupid—she knew something was up. She called me in the kitchen and said, "Young lady, either you've broken something valuable in the house, you've disgraced the family's good name, or it's report card day. Which is it?"

I was shaking in my shoes, thinking of all the punishment I was about to receive, as I handed her my report card. After a couple of long minutes of review, she finally said, "Well, I know I should be upset with you for not doing well in spelling, but the truth is I understand why you failed—because I am not good at spelling either."

At that moment a light went off in my head; no wonder I can't spell, *I have defective spelling genes!*

From that day on I had made a conscious decision that I was not good at spelling. I would go through the motions of trying to learn, but in truth I had made a decision that I would never be a good speller. So deep down inside of me I really didn't try very hard, or I'd learn only what I needed to to get a passing grade, or I'd just give up. In fact, looking back I realize I started bragging that I was not a good speller to justify my poor grades, but I was only reinforcing my belief that I could not spell.

When I was growing up, I did not understand that the words I used had an impact on me emotionally and on what I could accomplish in life. I had not been taught that I was a self-fulfilling prophecy—in other words, what I said and thought about myself would come true. It was as if I unconsciously believed that I could say negative things *about* myself, *to* myself, and those negative thoughts would have no effect on me or my future.

I am certain after you read my spelling story, you can identify some area in your life where you decided that you were not good at something and have never tried again to be better. We have created thoughts that evolved into beliefs and reinforced those beliefs until we *believe* them to be true. Scientists and behavioral experts agree that we use only a small fraction of our brain potential. One of the main reasons we use so little of our natural talents and potential is that we do not believe we have the ability to achieve our dreams and goals.

The purpose of this chapter is to coach you in experimenting with new strategies for expanding your personal power and winning back absolute control of your life. This information can give you the confidence and courage to make positive changes. You don't have to be a victim of life. You have the power to change strategies and create a happier life. However, you must be willing to accept total responsibility for changing your self-talk and the caliber of your thoughts about yourself and your potential.

As discussed in previous chapters, your brain is a computer. At birth our subconscious mind began to record every feeling, thought, and word that was spoken *to* you and *by* you. You accepted, without question, whatever information that your parents, teachers, and people in positions of authority told you. Generally, all that information was given out of love. However, keep in mind that these people were victims of others' beliefs and circumstances.

They were only human and did not have the resources we have today with self-help books, human potential training, and professional help. Remember that your influences also had weaknesses and negativity within them, which were passed on to you. The good news is that you have the power to override those limiting messages.

Shad Helmstetter, an expert on self-talk who authored *What to Say When You Talk to Yourself* and *The Self-Talk Solution*, wrote:

> Because 75 percent or more of our early programming was of the negative kind, we automatically followed suit with our own self talk—our own self-programming of the same negative kind. The result is that we grow to maturity with some of the most inappropriate and self-hindering programs imaginable stuck permanently in our subconscious minds, where they will affect every action we will ever take and every thought we will ever think, for the rest of our lives.

The bottom line is that we are now the sum total of all the programming others have given us, including the thoughts we have had about ourselves. So our brain is designed to make sure we live out the programs installed. The end result is that *all those past images, thoughts and directions will influence your attitudes and every action you take today*. If you do not take personal responsibility for the nurturing, care, and feeding of your own subconscious mind, you will be manipulated and controlled by past programming and your current environment.

You have the power to train your mind to choose what you think and not allow random thoughts to hold you hostage. *Your goal is to become inner-directed and focused, so that you decide what you want to think, rather than having your thoughts and emotions determined by the world around you.* The untrained mind has more emotional ups and downs because it is reacting to random thoughts.

It is believed that 40,000 to 50,000 thoughts enter your

mind every day. It has also been suggested that 80 percent of your thoughts are negative on an average day—can you imagine what your thoughts are like on a bad day? Moreover, what effect do those negative thoughts have on your attitude, your creativity, and your passion for life?

One of the most important discoveries in human development today is understanding the role our own casual thinking plays in shaping our lives and destiny. Historically we believed that thoughts were basically harmless bits of consciousness that held no substance or energy of their own. Neuroscientists, medical researchers, and psychologists have *proven* that thoughts are electrical impulses which trigger chemical activity in the brain. When you think, you are giving your brain an electrical command which responds by doing several things. The brain initially reacts by releasing chemicals into the body and directs the central nervous system to take any required action. Your thoughts also trigger the brain to scan its memory, searching out the appropriate file to record any necessary information about that thought that may be of future value.

The brain functions precisely as it is designed by receiving, processing, storing, and then acting on the information it was fed. Remember that your brain, like the earth, does not discern what you plant—it will work just as hard to grow weeds as it will beautiful flowers. Our goal in this chapter, with the skill of awareness, is to plant more beautiful, *empowering* thoughts so we can reap a more prosperous life.

Quite simply, we are self-fulfilling prophecies because the subconscious mind does not know the difference between *factual* reality and *imagined* reality. Many of your evolved beliefs have no foundation of truth, so, instead of promoting your purpose, they hold you back from success. If you *think* you are destined to be overweight, below average, poor, unlucky in love, clumsy, or even "not good at something," you will take actions that make these thoughts become reality. None of these thoughts are actually true, but thinking them creates beliefs and images in your mind, reinforcing these negative statements until they actually *become* true for you.

Human beings are creatures of habit. Our past programming forms our patterns of thinking. It is sad but true that the majority of our thoughts about ourselves hold us back from achieving the quality of life that is available to us. We are easily discouraged because, while we want to make changes in our habits, we soon painfully find out that willpower and *wishful* thinking does not work.

It is human nature to follow the path of least resistance. Accordingly, the mind also follows the habit of thoughts with the least resistance. That is why the old powerful programs in your mind overwhelm the new programs you are trying to establish. By taking charge of the caliber of information your feed your mind to create a new and more empowering program, you are literally *creating a new path* of least resistance for your mind to follow and operate from in the future.

Here is an example of how the subconscious mind, faced with making changes, brings two programs into conflict:

> You have been eating cookies and ice cream every night for three months and you have gained weight. You then decide you need to lose the extra weight and pass on the fattening treats at night. If you are human like the rest of us, you will find your willpower is very weak—as in, *"I'll start my diet for sure on Monday morning."*—and you will find reasons to justify why you can indulge in the treats just one more more night—like, *"This is a special occasion so it's okay to eat."* or *"Well, I'll just finish this last little bit so it won't go to waste!"*

Willpower does not work because the subconscious mind will attempt to act on the program which has the most power. In this case, the program that has the most power is the one to eat fattening foods every night. Once you understand *why* you have not been successful making changes in your life, you can use a new strategy to modify your behavior that will match the new desired goal.

To empower yourself to change a habit for the long term, you have to give your mind a new program that is stronger and more powerful. Your subconscious will immediately start to act on the new and stronger program. Then it becomes a matter of your subconscious mind trying to decide which program offers the path of least resistance. It will simply pursue the program that has the most energy, the more specific direction, and the most power.

We are not powerless to change ourselves. It is a well-established fact that your subconscious mind will accept and attempt to act on any information you give it, if you tell it often enough and strongly enough. The subconscious mind is a neutral machine which responds to information without subjective regard for its value in truth or accuracy. Repetition is the only secret you have to remember to overcome past programming. The simple fact is that the more often you present your subconscious mind with the same information, the more opportunities your subconscious mind will have to accept it.

A number of years ago, when I made a firm decision to become a professional speaker, I realized that I needed to convince or imprint on my subconscious mind that I was a great speaker and a great communicator if I was to become successful in my new career.

So I started saying to myself over and over again, *"I, Lee Milteer, am a good speaker."* In the back of my mind, my little voice inside would respond with *"LIAR!"* The reason for this was that, at the time, I was not a good speaker or a great communicator. But that was the desire and goal I had set for myself. As James Allen said, "Whatever we think about, we become." I set out to *think* myself into believing that I could capitalize on this talent I had discovered within myself. My challenge was to convince my mind to relax enough to start using my natural abilities.

So the statements I was using to attain this goal I began calling Declarations. I was declaring to myself my own power that I could be a good speaker—I could be a great communicator. The first person I had to convince of this ability would be myself. Over and over with great enthusiasm throughout the day, I would say to myself, *"I, Lee Milteer, now am a great speaker, I am a great communicator. I am becoming more and more successful every day, in every way, as a professional speaker."* I had to be able to *feel* like a good communicator before I could become one.

These statements are also known as Affirmations or auto-suggestions. These terms come about because the word Affirmation means to make firm. I prefer the term Declarations because I am declaring to myself, my subconscious, and to the world, what I am becoming. Wishful thinking has no effect or power other than to serve as a source of frustration for you at not getting what you want. When you declare you are going to do something, you are creating a new program in your mind, and, with repetition and action, this clear intention allows you to manifest new outcomes in your life!

The Formula For Making & Using Declarations Is Simple

1. Always use the present tense. Example: *"I am now a perfect size __ and weigh __lbs,"* instead of *"I want to be. . ."* or *"I wish I were. . ."*
2. Make your Declarations in the positive, rather than affirming what you don't want. Example: *"I now awaken on time bright and fresh,"* instead of *"I no longer oversleep."*
3. To make a greater impact on your subconscious and to make them easier to remember, keep your Declarations short and simple. Example: *"I am now patient and understanding with my family."*
4. Use Declarations that feel positive, expanding, and supportive. Only use declarations that *feel right to you.*
5. Create Declarations that focus on the "new." Embrace a spirit of creating something new, rather than changing or resisting current reality. Example: *"I enjoy the challenges of my new job."*
6. Act as if your Declarations are true. It is important to *give yourself permission* to believe your

Declarations are *true right now*. By allowing yourself to capture the feeling you'd experience with this new picture, you allow your mind to imprint a new and stronger picture on your subconscious mind. This tool allows you to achieve your goals faster.

7. Use your name in your Declaration whenever possible. This helps your subconscious mind accept a new picture of who you are becoming. Example: *"I, Your Name, am now filled with creative, exciting energy."*

8. When using your Declarations, make sure that your new programs have emotional force behind them. Emotion harnesses the extra energy you need to reprogram. The words are not as important as your feelings.

Strategies & Timing
For Using Declarations

1. Two of the most powerful times for your subconscious mind to reprogram itself are *before you get out of bed in the morning or just before you go to sleep at night.*

2. Use your Declarations in your *daily shower or bath.*

3. Use your Declarations while *driving* in your car.

4. State your Declarations *silently* also. Focus on your positive Declarations to improve your mood and attitude, instead of just letting your mind wander aimlessly.

5. *Use your Declarations aloud* throughout the day: while driving, dressing, exercising, and working around the house or yard.

6. *Put your Declarations on tape.* This gives your subconscious the opportunity to listen to your own voice. Your voice is the most powerful voice to your subconscious. I call these tapes "Self-Programming Commercials." The New Me!!!

7. *Write your Declarations.* Whenever you have any dead time, as in waiting for an appointment, write out a powerful Declaration eight to sixteen consecutive times. Focus your attention on the meaning of the words and *the feeling you get while writing.*

8. *Post your most powerful and important Declarations in places where you will see them frequently.* Including your desk, your refrigerator, your bathroom mirror, and/or the inside of your closet.

Using these techniques you will divest yourself of the encumbrance of others' beliefs, allowing you to become free to create the quality of life you deserve. These Declarations will help you gain enough confidence to step out on your own and discipline yourself to feel your own power to create whatever riches you want.

The Mind Likes Consistency!

I highly recommend you set up a 21-day regimen to create a new and positive habit, whereby you dedicate the same time each day to your inner growth so that a rhythm develops. For example, first thing in the morning just before you get up and become active is one of the most powerful times of the day, so make the most of it. Remember, what your mind focuses on, expands and sets the tone for your day. This is important in preventing yourself from being a reactor to life, letting the negative newspapers or radio and TV news determine your attitude for your day. Did you realize that experts in this field agree that 70 percent of the news in your daily newspaper is negative or fearful information? The really bad thing about this is that you don't consciously realize how your feelings and emotions are being impacted—*your subconscious mind will absorb everything to which it is exposed!* Instead of allowing your moods and emotions to be determined by the headlines, doesn't it seem like a more intellectual strategy to have planned out several declarations that empower you and enrich your day?

Design your Declarations to meet the needs of that day. This type of strategy allows you to use more of your potential and talents to deal with whatever you encounter. Every day is a new opportunity to start your brain's computer with programs that make you feel good and in control of your life.

The second time of day which you will find to be very powerful for programming your mind is just before you go to sleep. As you get comfortable and prepare yourself for sleep, begin repeating selected declarations to yourself until you naturally fall asleep. You will sleep better and awake in a better mood because you have installed information in your subconscious mind which is healing and soothing.

Have you ever noticed that, when you go to bed angry or frustrated, you tend to wake up with that same anger, or in a bad mood? This is your classic example of "garbage in - garbage out." The trick is to take charge of the caliber of information your brain settles on before you go to sleep.

A good place to use dead time to program yourself is in the shower. Start a wonderful ritual of saying your declarations out loud with great enthusiasm while enjoying your morning shower. You can even sing them! It is a safe place and no one can hear you.

Another ideal time and place is while driving in your car. The average person spends more than seven hours per week in their car. This presents a prime opportunity for saying your declarations out loud or even silently to yourself. By speaking in a deliberate or measured manner, the words you utter become symbols of your power. You will start to view yourself as a directed person in control of your life. It's a great strategy for using dead time and guaranteeing your future by reprogramming your mind.

Examples Of Declarations

(It is important to insert your name in your Declaration whenever possible so your subconscious knows who you are taking about!)

I (Your Name) NOW take full responsibility for my life and my thoughts.

I (Your Name) am NOW in control of my destiny and I am excited about the positive changes I am making in my life.

I (Your Name) NOW love and honor myself for who and what I am at this moment in time.

I (Your Name) NOW forgive and release myself from programming by others that does not serve me.

I (Your Name) NOW choose my future, rather than react to life's circumstances.

I (Your Name) NOW feel more confident and successful every day, in every way.

I (Your Name) am NOW practical and realistic and give myself the freedom to live my life to my fullest potential.

I (Your Name) NOW have drive, stamina, and a winning attitude.

Making any lasting change is not a one-stop process or overnight event because the brain is not designed to make sudden changes that will be permanent. Our brain is designed to follow patterns of habits and rules. We did not develop negative habits in one day and we cannot rid ourselves of these negative habits in a single attempt.

To empower yourself to make any long-term change, you must go to the core of yourself and *change your programming.* Simply trying to make changes in your life through external strategies will not change your programming. You must first make a clear decision about what you want changed. Then you will need to create a plan of action to override the past programming with new images and new empowering thoughts. The changes will start to happen because our brains have a more powerful program to follow.

In true self-management, your results change when your programs change. It is just as if you've been watching the same television show every night for the last five years; changing the channel and watching a new show brings you new information and new results.

A major benefit of changing your self-talk is in the power of overcoming negative habits. You become motivated and receptive to different perspectives on problems in your life, helping you set and achieve new goals. This empowers you to stop berating yourself.

Ultimately, you have to accept 100-percent responsibility for yourself and your future by controlling the caliber of information that you feed your brain's computer. It is futile to believe that other people or outside circumstances will take care of you. If you search deeply in your heart, you know that only you will really take care of you.

Taking full responsibility for your thoughts and actions is the true dividing line between successful and unsuccessful people. It is at the core of your success as an individual. *Being 100 percent responsible for yourself is essential to all worthwhile achievements and accomplishments of lasting value.*

Consider, for example, people who try to lose weight yet, each time they get within a few pounds of their goal, they lose motivation and regain all the weight. I have interviewed many people who have failed in achieving their goals just when the goal was finally in sight.

A few years ago, a good friend of mine, Sarah, decided to return to college and finish her degree. She had dropped out when she was younger to get married and have children, just *one month* before she would have graduated with her degree.

I was stunned to learn of this. I could not understand why she would just quit with mere days left before obtaining her goal. She explained at the time that she had lost interest in her studies, and, as her husband was doing very well in his business, there would be no need for her to work. Years went by until, one night over dinner, she finally confided the real reason she had dropped out.

Sarah had been afraid that, if she had her degree, people would expect her to do something worthy in the professional world. She further explained how she felt saying, "I did not feel I deserved any honors, because I remember my mother always telling me that a good woman's place was at home raising her children." I asked what kind of internal dialogue she had been using just before she quit, which had ultimately sabotaged her potential success.

Sarah became very sad and replied, "Well, I was telling myself how disappointed my mother would have been because I was not going to stay home full time and raise my children the way she did." Here's the clincher—*her mother had passed on several years before!*

My dear friend had allowed an old memory of her mother's values and beliefs to *keep her from her dreams.* She had continued to renew the power of old beliefs, long after she should have thrown them out and replaced them with new programs and beliefs that would have empowered her to reach her goals. Sarah also should have been aware of how her behavior was going to affect her children's future.

This true story clearly demonstrates how we can become our own worst enemy. All too often we do not give ourselves permission to break through the success barrier. We do not feel worthy of success because of programs in our brain's computer that were installed by *someone else's opinion*—an opinion by someone that we respected—which has been continually reinforced by our own self-talk.

One way to make progress in life is to first acknowledge what strategy we are currently using that is clearly not working. Take a moment now to think about what patterns or beliefs might be holding you back from your fullest potential or hindering pursuit of your dreams. Write down whatever thoughts or situations come to your mind.

To overcome or break through our success barrier, we have to *choose* to give our brain's computer new truths. We must replace or override old programs that were not true, even in the beginning.

As babies, we were not born with beliefs that hold us back from having the quality of life we really deserve. We collected them like excess baggage. We actually learned how to underestimate our talents, our strengths, and our potential.

By reinforcing any outdated beliefs, we are continuing to nurture them, making it harder for us to change our future.

Pattern Interrupts: What Do You Say to Yourself When You Have Made a Mistake or Reinforced a Belief that Holds You Back?

Many of us browbeat ourselves, and destroy our self-esteem in the process, by being so hard on ourselves. I recommend that you treat yourself like you would your very best friends. When they make mistakes, you don't berate them with how foolish they are. You reassure them, telling them it's okay and encourage them to do better next time. So why be so hard on yourself? The bottom line is this: just as you are nurturing and loving to your dearest friends, you must be nurturing and loving to yourself and your subconscious mind, if you want to improve your future.

To aid you in this there is a wonderful technique called a "Pattern Interrupt." When your actions or performance does not meet your expectations, don't belittle yourself with negative self-talk. This type of response will only perpetuate the poor performance you did not want from the beginning and will add to the negative programming. You will find that using this new tool will empower you to emphasize to your subconscious mind new and positive messages or programs. You must replace those images of yourself that do not create value in your life and which you certainly do not want to continue.

As an example: How many times have you caught yourself saying *"I am always late?"* Now think about what you are programing yourself to be—LATE! In the future, instead of reinforcing the negative habit, say to yourself: *"CANCEL, THAT'S NOT LIKE ME, NEXT TIME I'LL. . ."*

Then you want to follow up immediately with statements to your subconscious mind to imprint a new program. In this case, *"That's not like me to be late. I always leave ten minutes early and I am always on time."*

Saying this once obviously won't ensure your timeliness in the future. It is a statement you will have to consciously and repeatedly program into your life over a period of time for the information to be assimilated. Your brain's computer must digest and absorb the new program. When you use this technique, you are literally taking the four volts of electrical energy in your brain and creating a new program.

A few years ago, while I was sitting in the Hartsfield International Airport in Atlanta, a woman by the name of Barbara rushed up to me saying how delighted she was to see me. She continued with, "I wanted to let you know that the information you share in your seminars about Pattern Interrupts really improved my marriage." Naturally at this point she had my curiosity very piqued and I inquired "How so?" Here is her story:

> Barbara explained that she had attended my seminar the year before. There, I had gone over in detail how important it is to not reinforce the negative, but rather to literally program with our words what behavior we want.
>
> After my seminar she went home and began preparing dinner in the kitchen. Her husband Joe was in the den watching television with their three sons. At this point she inserted, "I want you to know I love my husband, he's a wonderful father, a wonderful provider; I'm very lucky to have him. However, he has a terrible temper and in the past I unconsciously and unknowingly reinforced his own view of himself by saying— *'That's just like you Joe, you always fly off the handle and lose your temper.'"*
>
> That day I decided to use your strategy on him. I calmly went into the den where they were watching football just as the television station cut in for a newsbreak in the middle of the game. My husband reacted with his usual ranting, raving, screaming, and hollering, and I suddenly realized why my three sons were having temper tantrums—they were emulating their father!
>
> With all the sincerity I could muster at the moment, I looked Joe deeply in the eyes and said, *"Now Joe, that's not like you to lose your temper, you're*

usually so calm and even-minded." He looked at me like I'd lost my mind! Over the next nine months I didn't realize how much I used this phrase, *"That's not like you"* whenever Joe lost his temper.

One day we decided to go out to a fancy restaurant for a celebration where we sat and sat, waiting for our food to be delivered. I noticed Joe was becoming angrier and angrier, his face getting red; he was clearly getting upset at the length of time we'd been waiting to be served. As I realized he was going to lose his temper and make a scene, I simply closed my eyes and waited for the outburst.

At that moment, I spotted the waitress coming toward our table with the food and, to my surprise, my husband turned to me and said, "You know Honey, that's really not like me to lose my temper."

Barbara didn't realize how effective this new strategy had been until two weeks after the restaurant incident. She and her sons were outside one day and she actually overheard her youngest son say to one of the neighbor's boys, *"Tommy, that's not like you to steal my toys!"*

After she told me this story, we both laughed at its conclusion. It was amazing how she had consistently given her husband new information about himself, and now she could finally see a new Joe! I think the moral here is that we all have an opportunity, not only to improve ourselves, but also to influence those people around us whom we care about.

This story reinforces the message in the very popular book, *The One Minute Manager* by Ken Blanchard and Spencer Johnson. One of the book's strongest points is about catching people doing things right, instead of reinforcing people's negative habits.

Whether we acknowledge it or not, we are influencing people around us on a daily basis. Since it is proven that our self-image is created by our environment, why not benefit others by looking for, finding, and reaffirming what they do right? In this manner, instead of reinforcing negative programs to those around us, we can hopefully add some positive reinforcement. Alex Haley, author of *Roots* and one of the world's most celebrated writers, used to say, "Find the good in people and *praise it.*"

The Negative Past Does Not Create Your Future Unless You Give It Permission To Do So

One of our culture's favorite pastimes is to dredge up any and all emotional pain of previous negative experiences, bad luck stories, failed relationships, and/or physical ailments. Dwelling on these past failures and injustices uses your electrochemical or mental energy and *recreates the same bad experience* in your subconscious mind! This in turn gives it more power to make us feel bad or unworthy.

When I lived at home as a child, whenever something bad happened to me, my mother used to say, *"You cannot move forward successfully if your head is turned looking backwards."* That's a very true statement. The choices we make every day give us the ability to focus our mental energy on whatever we choose. We can either dwell on the past or *move beyond it and focus on the future.*

ALL energy has effects. What you focus on expands. Focusing on past painful events has a profound effect on what your future will be. Any time you dwell on your past failures or inadequacies, you only create more fear about your opportunities in the future.

You'll remember the old saying, "This is the first day of the rest of your life." Well, it's true! The past is a locked door. No matter how hard you may try, you cannot go back and change it. *Your point of power is in the present*—it is what you do with your present time and energy. Your future is created by the thoughts and energy you use today. It is *always* up to you to give yourself permission to stop talking about and thinking about what happened in the past. Focus your mental, physical, and emotional life energy on what you are going to create in the future.

What your future will look like is totally dependent on what information and self-direction you give yourself with your self-talk. It is a practiced skill to learn to be able to choose what thoughts come into your mind, rather than be ruled by the thoughts that flow at random. You must recognize that you have the power of control to master your inner dialogue. To make your mind *obey* you rather than *control* you. What an awesome feeling to realize that *your future is up to you!* Your thoughts create your reality!

_6_

DREAM BIG:
BECOME A VISIONARY

Florence Chadwick's goal was to become the first woman ever to swim from France to England. For years she trained and disciplined herself to keep swimming long after her body cried out for relief. In 1952 the big day came: she set out full of hope, surrounded by news media, well-wishers in small boats, and of course the skeptics who doubted she'd make it.

As she neared the coast of England, a heavy fog settled in and the waters became increasingly cold and choppy. From a nearby craft, her mother encouraged her, "Come on, Florence, you can make it! It's only a few more miles!"

Finally exhausted beyond belief, she regretfully asked to be pulled aboard the boat—not knowing she was just a few hundred yards from her goal. She felt defeated and heartbroken at not reaching her dream, especially when she discovered how close she had been. Later, she told reporters, "I'm not offering excuses, but I think I could have made it if I had been able to see my goal."

Not surprisingly, Florence Chadwick decided to try again. This time, she concentrated on developing a mental image of the coast of England. She memorized every feature of the distant coast and fixed it clearly in her mind. On the appointed day, she encountered all the choppy waters and the fog that she had met before, but this time she made it.

Two-time Olympic pentathlete Marilyn King said, "If you can't imagine it, you can't ever do it. In my experience the image always precedes the reality." She provides a very moving example of how powerful the conscious use of picturing what you want can be. When Marilyn King was preparing for the 1980 Olympic trials, she suffered a severe back injury and was confined to bed just nine months before the time trials. Determined not to let this injury keep her from performing, she spent the next four months doing nothing but watching films of the best performers in the pentathlon events and visualizing herself going through the same events.

After she placed second at the Olympic trials despite her lack of physical preparation, she stated that it was her psychological state, not her physical condition, that gained her victory. Thomas Edison once said, "Good fortune is what happens when opportunity meets with preparation."

My first big break as a professional speaker came when I was retained to speak to a group of more than a thousand employees for AT&T in New Jersey. I had been speaking to very small groups up to that point, and 1,000 people was clearly beyond my comfort zone. The truth was, I felt scared out of my mind!

I went to see my mentor, a woman twenty-five years older than I, with much wisdom and life experience. I told her how every time I even thought of standing in front of 1,000 people my hands started to sweat, my knees shook, and my stomach didn't know if it was going to have diarrhea or nausea! She laughed at this statement and injected some humor into my situation by saying, "Did you know the number one fear, for all of North America's professionals, is public speaking? Have you ever seen the fear list? Public speaking actually beats out snakes and death! Can you believe that people wrote down they would rather die or handle snakes before standing in front of a group to speak!"

She went on to say that if you were to ever be truly successful in life, you had to stop buying into limiting mass belief systems, such as the belief that speaking before a large group is fearful. Check things out for yourself. Just because "they" say something is difficult or impossible, doesn't make it true. By the way, who are "they" anyway? And why are you listening to them? It's clear that "they" are the people who have failed at what they say can't be done.

My mentor's final advice to me was the best I've ever gotten from anyone. She said to me, "If you don't mentally, physically, and emotionally prepare yourself for an opportunity, that opportunity will go to someone else who *is* prepared. Visualize yourself in front of those 1,000 people and only see the end result that you want to happen."

Taking her advice, I went to the library and checked out all the books I could on a technique called visualization. It's also called mental rehearsal, guided imagery, self-hypnosis, behavior modification; scientists refer to it as imprinting. I found that the bottom line is using your imagination—it is the workshop of the mind. Everything man-made had to be created in the mind before it could manifest into reality.

So for the next thirty days, I followed the instructions I had read about how to use mental rehearsal. When I first woke in the morning, I stayed in bed for an extra five minutes and imagined myself standing in front of those 1,000 people. I saw myself as a confident speaker, knowing all the facts and answering all questions professionally. I then "saw" the end result that I wanted—the group clapping enthusiastically after I finished. In the evening, just before I went to sleep, I played the same scene over and over in my mind, creating as many details as possible of the sights, sounds, and feelings.

During this thirty-day period, I also did the tangible work of practicing my presentation, anticipating possible questions, and outlining what I wanted to share with the group. In other words, I did my homework. My favorite motto is that it is better to be over-rehearsed than ambushed!

The day of my speech, I was nervous and had wild butterflies. But within two minutes of starting my speech, my comfort zone, which had always been with small groups, expanded. I now felt comfortable in front of 1,000 people! I had rehearsed in my mind over sixty times prior to that moment, literally seeing myself speaking long before I got there. I expected to do a great job and I did. What you expect in life often becomes reality.

This experience helped shape my future because, for the

first time, I realized the power of the mind and what I could create. This eye-opening experience has guided me from that day to where I am today. I realize I could have never had the confidence to go for the goals in my life without the help of mental rehearsal. This tool allowed me to break through barriers that I had set up in my own mind of what I could and could not do.

The best way to prepare for anything in life is to visualize success. Your imagination is your own personal workshop of the mind. In it, you can see all the possibilities of the future and exactly how to go about creating those dreams. You can rehearse the possibilities and create plans and visualize ways to succeed, all in the privacy of your mind. Visualization is using the mind to create a better existence.

This tool has actually been known, used, and explored since the beginning of time. The Roman philosopher Marcus Aurelius said, "Our life is what our thoughts make it." Walt Disney said, "If you can dream it, you can do it." Everything we create in the physical world starts as an idea.

Today, a growing variety of people use this powerful tool to create better lives for themselves. Business people, athletes, teachers, physicians, psychotherapists, and even dieters find visualization very powerful. The mind is far more resourceful and complicated than we have ever recognized. Winston Churchill said, "The empires of the future are the empires of the mind."

A study of high-powered executives was done by researchers at Stanford, Yale, and Harvard universities. It found that a shared trait among "super achievers" was the ability to sense what they wanted before they got it. These "super achievers" have the ability to translate their ideas or goals into actual physical visions; they create pictures of what they want down to the smallest detail. Knowing exactly what they want, they can see it, taste it, smell it, and even imagine the emotions and sounds associated with the main desires or goals. Their sharp sensory vision allows them to pre-live their goals before they become realities.

Dr. Charles Garfield, author of *Peak Performers*, said,

"There can be no question that mental rehearsal of future events brings results." He went on to say that "Our culture has widespread skepticism and even disbelief, about the power of mental rehearsal. We trust the brain's logical functioning much more than its imaginative functioning. But among the peak performers we studied, both forms of gathering knowledge were strongly developed. Mental rehearsal can provide a tremendous boost to performance; we know that as a fact."

Other research shows that mental practice has the same effect as real practice. Former Dallas Cowboys all-star defensive back Bill Bates agrees: "The night before the New York Giants game, I had an image where I saw myself pulling in two interceptions. I saw it all in my mind—every play and my every move. The next day, I got those interceptions and both were crucial. Would I have gotten them anyway? I don't know. But I do know I got them."

Visualization can be used in all areas of your life, from attaining your life's dream goal to rehearsing for a job interview or a speech. This tool can help you reduce the effects of stressful situations such as asking for a raise, coping with difficult people, losing weight, quitting smoking, improving relationships—both personal and professional—and performing better at sports. All of these areas in your life can benefit from imagery. It doesn't matter what level your goals are on: physical, emotional, mental, or spiritual.

Most world-class athletes utilize mental rehearsal, according to Jack Nicklaus, who said, "Good golf is 50 percent physical coordination and 50 percent mental rehearsal." Nicklaus notes in his book *Golf My Way*, "I never hit a shot, not even in practice, without having a very sharp, in-focus picture of it in my head. It's like a color movie; first I 'see' the ball where I want it to finish, nice and white and sitting high on the bright green grass. Then the scene quickly changes and I 'see' the ball going there: its path, trajectory, and shape, even its behavior on landing. Then there is a sort of fade-out and the next scene shows me making the kind of swing that will turn the previous images into reality." Visualization can improve motor skills and muscle memory.

A movie star with one of the biggest box-office draws, Arnold Schwarzenegger said, "The mind is the limit. As long as the mind can envision the fact that you can do something, you can do it—as long as you really believe 100 percent." He also said, "I used weights to tone my body, but I used my mind to shape it."

According to Dr. David Thornburg, who teaches creativity at Stanford's business school, "In mental rehearsal you're engaging your subconscious as an ally in pursuit of goals. With imaging reinforcing the goals' importance, the subconscious will put that goal very high on your priorities, making it far more likely that you'll unconsciously begin adjusting your actions in ways that will make that goal happen for you." The mind is a marvelous tool. When freed, it will find so many ways for us to achieve what we want.

The power of visualization, backed by sincere commitment, has helped many cancer patients. Dr. Carl Simonton, a Dallas oncologist, has pioneered an approach that reinforces standard medical treatment with mental imagery. Dr. Simonton says that cancer patients can influence their immune systems to become more active in fighting the illness. The patients practice visualizing the cancer as weak cells and visualize the body's white blood cells as powerful strong cells hunting down the weak cells to kill them. By doing this three times each day, they create some type of either realistic or symbolic images to kill the cancer in their body. One patient saw his good cells as a "pac man" eating all the cancer cells! Dr. Simonton's former patients have reported promising results with this technique.

Doctors say that because of biofeedback science, we can use visualization to change the rate of our heartbeat and other body functions by what we are feeling and thinking. Our outer experience is directly connected to our inner experience.

Using mental rehearsal is not just for adults; children can benefit from this tool to help them improve in school.

After one of my seminars on how to use mental rehearsal as a resource to improve potential, I received an exciting letter from a man named Thomas who lived in Texas. He wrote that he was a single parent who had been having problems with his ten-year-old son and his school math work. He wrote to say how he had taught his son the technique of using visualization.

Thomas actually "dared" his son to mentally rehearse what it would be like if he could get good grades in math, see himself getting A's on tests, and see the praise from the teacher. He felt, "If my son cannot imagine getting a passing grade in math, he won't even make the attempt to try." The father ended the letter with a very positive report: "Once my son started to mentally see himself pulling that impossible grade, he started paying more attention in class, doing his homework, asking for extra help. I am proud to say his grades have gone from low D's to a high B."

It's clear that with a mental rehearsal breakthrough under their belts, children are far more receptive to mastering the practical tools for realizing their new ambitions. Once children or adults grasp that potential is only a state of mind, they can replace the old negative views of themselves with new scripts of success. There is nothing to stop them, because once you imagine something new for yourself, you begin to be flooded with ideas about how to realize that image. You begin to get excited with possibilities. All this will come about when you have allowed yourself to break through your own worst barrier: what you believe are your capabilities.

Counselors and therapists who recommend visualization say it is the true key to tap into your potential. Their research reveals that all of our skills are learned through the image-making process, whether it's driving a car, reading a book, or dressing yourself. You use your mind to picture the activity before you actually perform it. Think of it like this: your mind works like a movie projector, screening an endless reel of memories, daydreams, and scenes of situations both real and imagined. You have the power to direct your movie projector (your mind) to reach your desired goals.

There is more to visualization than mental rehearsal or suggestion. Our nervous system reacts to mental images in the same way it reacts to images from the external world, so the nervous system cannot tell the difference between an imagined experience and a real experience. I would like to give you a couple of examples to prove this point. Have you ever been in a state where your mind was just wandering and you started to remember a time that you really were embarrassed? You started to remember all the things that happened and how you felt. The more you thought of this situation, the faster your heart started to beat, your armpits started to sweat, you relived the emotions of that long-past situation.

This occurs because the subconscious and nervous system cannot tell the difference between an imagined situation and the real thing! That is why you suffered stress again over an event in the past and most likely long gone. Another powerful example to prove the power of your imagination: all human beings have sexual fantasies that are part of our natural state. The next time you have a sexual fantasy notice how your imagination affects your body and how your body responds.

Thoughts are our most powerful tools. We can create a rich life filled with love, rewarding work, satisfying relationships, health, financial prosperity, inner peace, and harmony. The use of creative visualization gives us a magical key to tap into the natural goodness and richness of life. Creative visualization is magic in the truest sense of the word because it involves aligning the natural principles of our conscious and subconscious mind with the universal mind that connects to all life.

I believe that our physical universe is made up of energy. The objects that appear to be solid and separate from each other in the way our physical senses perceive them are really just made up of particles that eventually turn out to be simply pure energy. We are all part of a large energy field. All forms of energy are interrelated and can affect one another. Energy vibrates at different rates of speed and light with different qualities, from very fine to very dense.

Matter is considered to be compact energy and is relatively dense; therefore, it is slower to move and change. A perfect example would be a rock; even a rock is changed over time because of the natural energies of water, light, and wind. On the other hand, our thoughts, which are made of very light, fine forms of energy, are very easy and quick to change. So, by using our thoughts, we can affect our outside world.

It's an established universal law that like attracts like. The same principle holds true with energy, which is magnetic—energy of a certain vibration attracts energy of a similar vibration. Therefore thoughts and feelings have their own magnetic energy which always attract energy of the same nature. For example, positive-thinking people tend to attract other positive-thinking people; negative people seem to be attracted to other negative thinkers.

We are always creating our reality from our thoughts. Our thoughts act like blueprints of the image we want to create. The image magnetizes and guides the physical energy to flow into the form we have imagined and allows us to manifest our desires into reality. Metaphysicians call visualization the Law of Radiation and Attraction. This is simply the principle that as you sow, so shall you reap, in your thoughts and in your life. We always attract into our lives whatever we strongly believe, think about, or imagine most vividly.

The more you use the unlimited power of the mind to visualize what you want, the more your new programs can manifest in your life. Keep in mind that there are no limits except the limits you put on yourself. You have the power, through your thoughts and imagination, to break through any barriers holding you back from a rich life.

Please do not confuse visualization with daydreaming or fantasizing. Although both involve the use of your imagination, it's only when you commit yourself to a goal that you can truly take advantage of visualization. Daydreams and fantasies are usually unrealistic thoughts that we really don't expect to actually happen or have little investment in, such as winning the lottery or marrying a movie star.

It's important to point out that visualization or mental imagery is not a method of self-deception; it is one of the strongest tools known to date for self-direction and tapping into your potential. By becoming the star, director, editor, and writer of the picture of your life, you are synthesizing the experience of your success in your mind. The vision acts like a magnet; once the image is fixed in the mind, your subconscious is alerted to bring about factors that will help you achieve the goal you just programmed. In time, our deliberate visions become self-fulfilling. Dr. Bernie Zilbergeld, psychologist and author of *Mind Power*, said, "In a nutshell, mental training is simply a way of reprogramming the mind to achieve more positive behaviors, feelings, and results."

You have the ability to create movies in your mind and you do it with total perfection. You do it every time you think of someone or remember something or even daydream. Without your being aware of it, you create pictures in your mind in countless different situations every day. As an example, try choosing an object near you, examine it in detail, note its shape, color, and size. After you have examined it, close your eyes and picture in your mind what you just saw. If you can do that, you've just proved to yourself how you can direct your imagination. How we all use our inner movie screen differs slightly. Some people see their pictures in color, while others see them in black and white. There is no right or wrong way. Any way that you sense and feel your images are just perfect for you.

The more you practice using visualization, the better your brain can become at directing what happens in your daily life. This allows you to be in more control of your experiences. By using visualization, we can create a state of awareness in which we are not using our logical, linear, or analytical thinking in our experiences, but are actually experiencing through feeling.

Basic Steps for Using Visualization

First, if you think of the mind as a computer, you will want to program this computer correctly. The best way to begin using the power of visualization is to first get your computer into the correct mode for programming. This correct mode is to be deeply relaxed both in body and mind. It's only when you are relaxed that your mind will open to fresh ideas and new techniques. When your mind and body are deeply relaxed, your brain actually becomes slower; this slower state is known as the alpha state.

Research in this area has found that, for the practical purposes of using visualization, during this relaxed time our subconscious records new programs more effectively. Two of the most effective times to use visualization are as you awaken in the morning—while your mind and body are very relaxed and receptive—and at night just before sleeping. Experts also agree that having your body in a position so the spine is straight will help you come into the alpha state faster. You can also do this by sitting in a comfortable chair in a quiet place in the middle of the day, to relax and renew yourself by playing your own mind's movies.

The second step for effective visualization is having a clearly defined goal of whatever you would like to have or create in your life. You must have the faith and belief that you can realize your goal.

The third step is to create a mental picture as if the goal were already yours; act as if the picture were real today, not some time in the future. Be sure to fill in the small details of the sights, colors, smell, textures, and feelings; the more realistic the detailing the better. If you can see, hear, touch, smell, and taste your goal, your picture will be that much clearer and will work that much better. The more realistic the images the better the results. Imagine yourself with the goal or in the situation as you desire. Do not reinforce negative pictures. It's very important to see what you want so you imprint the new pictures in your subconscious mind.

The fourth step is to focus on your mental picture as often as possible. Do this at least twice a day for five to ten minutes each time for 21 days. Research has proven that it takes a minimum of 21 days to effect any perceptible change in a mental image. It takes only three weeks for an old mental image to dissolve and a new mental image to form.

By clearly focusing on what you want to create, you make this new image become an integral part of you—you start to live as if you've already achieved the goals or dreams that you were visualizing.

The fifth step is to have, if possible, a tangible picture of the goals you are consciously creating. From various sources, such as magazines or newspapers, start to collect the symbols for what you want to create in your life. These symbols can be in the form of pictures, sayings, or statements that represent the goals and dreams in your life.

Put them in a place where you can see them several times every day to reinforce your true wants and desires.

Be a Visionary for Your Own Future

I had the honor of doing some seminars for the Walt Disney organization in Florida a few years ago. While I was there, a manager of one of the resort hotels told me this story.

A few years after Disney passed away, the beautiful Epcot Center was finished and opened to the public. A group of foreign exchange students were visiting, enjoying themselves, and admiring how wonderful it was. A vice president of the Disney organization happened to walk by and overheard one of the students say, "It really upsets me that Disney never got to see Epcot." The vice president turned around and said to the group: "You don't understand. It's because Disney saw it, that it is here today!"

My favorite quote of all time is from Helen Keller: "The greatest tragedy in life is people who have sight but no vision." One of the secrets of success is to not work so hard with your physical sweat; instead use your mind to work out the details of how to be the person you want to be. The difference between average people and outstanding people is the degree of motivation within them. Are you motivated to spend ten minutes a day envisioning the future you want to create for yourself? By deliberately visualizing the experience of success in your mind, you can turn aspirations into realities. Dare to break away from the old, and create an exciting and rewarding future for yourself.

CHAPTER
-7-
INTUITION:
YOUR SECRET TALENT

"The mind can only proceed so far upon what it knows, and can prove. There comes a point where the mind takes a leap—call it intuition or what you will—and comes out on a higher plane of knowledge."
—Albert Einstein

Intuition is called many things—gut feeling, a hunch, sixth sense, instinct, a strong feeling, the eye of the mind. It speaks to you through insights, revelations, and urges. Intuition, listening to that inner part of yourself, is clearly one of the most important areas to develop in your life if you are interested in success, prosperity, and happiness. Intuition goes beyond that which is known into the unknown. Intuition can help you make financial decisions, be a better manager or parent, and capitalize on opportunities. It's a natural human function and your closest advisor. Most of your knowledge is book-learned and much of that is outdated and obsolete. Logic and analysis can lead you only half the way to a good decision. The next step frequently requires using your intuitive powers; pay attention and rely on that internal part of yourself, that voice inside that tells you when things feel right.

As we discussed earlier in this book, the subconscious mind remembers everything it has ever heard, read, seen, or been exposed to with your five senses. It's an enormous memory bank that will respond to your every request. When you ask it questions, your subconscious mind goes into a search mode, finding the information to supply your conscious mind the answer. Your intuition, however, can analyze large masses of data and make a judgmental decision all in one step.

It is interesting that in our western culture we seem to comprehend almost all of our experiences through the logical, linear, analytical thinking process. We use words to communicate this kind of thinking. Because words are our way of understanding our world, we've almost forgotten we have an intuitive, creative part of ourselves. We have been programmed to be so logical and analytical in our thinking, that we forget our intuitive abilities. We're not trained to say *I feel* but rather *I think*. If we deny and cut off our intuition, then we get trapped by concepts learned through our programmed minds. Yesterday's learned beliefs cannot solve today's challenges or enable us to capitalize on tomorrow's opportunities.

We've all been conditioned by society since birth that, if you cannot relate to something with your five senses, that is see, touch, taste, hear, or feel it, it must not exist. Even our educational system values only analytical processes of thinking. Very little attention or support is given to those students with creative or artistic talents in our public school system. So it's no surprise that, with all the past programming, we're afraid to trust those thoughts or feelings that sometimes just "come to us" as having valuable information. Only by learning to trust that inner knowledge can you really use your true potential in life. Our life styles have accelerated and, many times, there is not time to do all the fact-finding to make a logical decision. We must learn to seize the moment and listen to our inner wisdom.

Today more and more successful people—executives, artists, entrepreneurs, and homemakers—are realizing that making decisions is not an exclusive function of the analytical left side of the brain. You must now use the intuitive and creative right side of your brain as well. You must have an integration of analytical and creative, intuitive thinking. This theory is commonly referred to as "whole brain thinking."

Dr. Jonas Salk, developer of the polio vaccine, said, "Intuition will tell the thinking mind where to look next." In his book *Anatomy of Reality: Merging of Intuition and Reason,* Salk said, "A new way of thinking is now needed to deal with our present reality. Our subjective responses (intuitive) are more sensitive and more rapid than our objective responses (reasoned). This is the nature of the way the mind works. We first sense, and then we reason why."

In *Psychology Today*'s June 1993 issue, Daniel Cappon, M.D., wrote, "Although a trained scientist and great believer in rational thought, I am convinced that intuition is the older, wiser, and perhaps greater part of human intelligence." He went on to say, "Intuition has always been a vital part of human intelligence. It encompasses skills that have always been critical to human life. In a sense, intuition is responsible for the survival of the species."

Dr. Cappon became the first full-time professor for the York University's Environmental Arts and Sciences Department in Toronto. Their goal is to protect the health of humans and the environment by preventing its many hazards. He said, "Although a scientist, I became increasingly familiar with the limitations of science and its application to such problems. Fact-based, deductive, and analytical thinking is usually too late, often occurring after the fact. Nor is it sensitive to circumstance, contradictions, or the complexity and variability of human nature, most especially, relationships. It is simply not enough for the many challenges and constancy of change of modern life."

Astronaut Edgar Mitchell, a doctor of science from MIT, former U.S. Navy captain, and the sixth man on the moon, said this: "Man's potential knowledge is more than the product of his five senses." He speaks with passion of the "mysterious, creative process that works outside our conscious awareness." Dr. Mitchell believes intuition is the way we can solve our most difficult problems. While preparing for a lunar flight, Mitchell said, "We spent ten percent of our time studying plans for the mission and ninety percent learning how to react intuitively to all the 'what ifs.' Reliance on the intuitive response, was the most important part of this astronaut's training."

Trusting your intuition will often mean taking a risk; many times you will not be able to find rational reasons for doing what you *feel* you should. It has been taught to us by all the great teachers of mankind—listen to the inner you. All answers are within your own self.

I have lived my life with great success by use of my intuition, doing what I feel I should do versus what my brain or others told me was the right thing to do. I have painfully learned that if I do not listen to my inner voice, I nearly always regret my actions.

How many times have you left home in the morning when it was beautiful outside, the sun was shining, and the forecast was for a clear day? Yet something inside of you kept saying, take a raincoat or umbrella. You ignored your inner nudging and, before the end of the day, it was pouring! How many times have you hired someone or bought something when you knew it was not going to work out, but you went through with it anyway?

I had an experience like this once when I needed to find a replacement for my business manager. I interviewed for days and became very frustrated at trying to find the right person to fit the job. I was about to leave for a speaking tour that would last several weeks and desperately needed someone to run my office while I was gone. I interviewed someone who looked fabulous on paper; she had worked for someone in my business before and had great references, but somehow I *knew I* should not hire her. However, logically everything seemed perfect; I didn't listen to my inner voice, my intuition, and hired her anyway. Within two weeks, while I was out of town, she left my office and never bothered to return, leaving my business in chaos. I sincerely learned my lesson about hiring people: if I don't *feel* good about them, I won't hire them, regardless of their credentials.

One of the first and most remarkable times that I was forced to acknowledge my intuition was on New Year's Day in 1981. I was preparing to move into a new house and I had borrowed a van to personally pack my most valuable belongings, my china, crystal, silver, art, etc. I had friends over helping me load up the van when they decided to leave and pick up something to eat. When they returned, they asked, "Where's the van? It's all loaded, what did you do with it?" When I ran out to the front of my house, I could not believe my eyes—the van had been stolen with all my personal treasures. My friends called the police, and, as we waited restlessly for them to arrive, I went upstairs to my bedroom, closed the door and just sat down on the floor. I was stunned; I couldn't believe this had happened! I asked myself where could that van be; how can I do something to get it back? I had closed my eyes when suddenly, for not more than two seconds, I saw the van in my mind and saw exactly where it was. At that instant in time, I *knew* where the van was; I saw it in a graveyard about two miles from my home. It was almost dark at the time, this graveyard was in a very bad section of town, and it wasn't safe for us to go over there after dark.

As soon as the police came to take the report, I asked them to please go check out the graveyard. I explained that I had a feeling that was where the van was, and, if they hurried maybe they could catch the thieves. To put it mildly, they thought I was crazy and just wrote up the report. Two days later the police called me to say they found the van, stripped down and empty in the graveyard that I had told them about.

How did I know where that van was? To this day I can't explain it. All that I know is that experience taught me to pay a lot more attention to my intuition than I ever had before. A few months later, I encountered another situation that allowed me to test the reliability of listening to my intuition. I was scheduled to fly to Florida, but, when I arrived at the airport, my flight had been canceled. Naturally everyone rushed to book the next flight leaving in the next hour. As we were standing in line, my inner voice told me to get out of that line and go to another airline to book a flight. I checked into this other airline's flight; it was leaving two hours later and arriving much later. This didn't make logical sense to me but I could afford the time and I was still in awe over the stolen van episode. That made me willing to check out my intuition, so I booked the later flight on the other airline. As it turned out, it was a good thing I listened to my intuition; the flight for which I had originally been in line was also canceled, and I wouldn't have made it that night if I had not taken a chance and listened to my intuition to use another airline.

I recommend that you have some fun in life and start testing your intuitive abilities. When the phone rings, ask yourself who it is before you answer—see how many times you're right. When waiting for an elevator, guess which one will come first. There are dozens of small games you can play with yourself to strengthen your abilities. Your intuitive "muscle" gets stronger as you use it which will increase your percentage of accurate information. Then, when you really need your intuition, you will feel more confident in using it.

Author Philip Goldberg wrote in his book *The Intuitive Edge* about the ". . .astonishing speed with which the truly intuitive mind can bring together bits of information only remotely related in time and meaning to form the sudden hunch or whispered feeling that we call intuition."

Since successful management is an inexact science, most business executives secretly prize their intuition. It's the art of making decisions with insufficient information. John Naisbitt's best selling book *Megatrends* confirms, "Another shift I see that really impresses me is a new respectability for intuition in corporate settings. Now people are willing to say, 'I just feel this is going to work out.'"

Mary Kay Ash recalls how she was almost disastrously misled by an articulate but largely incompetent marketing expert as she was beginning her cosmetics company in 1963. This man, whom she had agreed to hire, sounded like a marketing whiz with enthusiastic plans for launching Mary Kay Cosmetics into the marketplace. One day, as she stood talking to this man outside her office, she suddenly changed her mind. She said, "I had no reason, just intuition." She added that within six months she was thrilled with her decision, when she found out this man had been indicted on a felony. Conrad Hilton, who was well known for using his intuition in his hotel business, wrote the book *Be My Guest.* In it he stated, "I know when I have a problem and have done all I can to figure it out, I keep listening in a sort of inside silence till something clicks and I feel a right answer."

One of my favorite books is Richard Bach's *Jonathan Livingston Seagull.* This book would have never been the success it is today if Eleanor Friede, a Macmillan editor, had not listened to her intuition and taken action. Friede had contacted Bach about publishing his future work when he told her about a little book which had been turned down by over two dozen publishing houses. "My agent thinks it's a children's book, but I don't," he told her, and asked if she'd like to read it. She took it to her beach house that weekend and read it early one morning on the deck beside the ocean. She knew immediately she had to publish it, not by rational planning, but because of the way it made her feel. Intuitively. She also knew the hard part would be to persuade the editorial board to publish and then to keep it going. The book was published in the fall of 1970; a first printing of 7,500 copies was gone by early December. It was a fight to get the second printing, with the Christmas sale past. But she got it, the first of many reprintings. The book eventually became the number-one bestseller in America for two years, 1972 and 1973, and is still an all-time bestseller worldwide.

Ours is a world where science has succeeded in explaining most observable phenomena, making it hard for many to accept as real anything that is unexplained. Many times you can personally experience some instance of mental telepathy and still consider it just a coincidence. Physicists and psychologists say there is evidence of an energy link between everything in the universe. Everything that happens is simultaneously encoded in this energy pattern. If this is true, it would make telepathy and clairvoyance more plausible and certainly give us a deeper understanding of how intuition works. This would explain why animals run away when anticipating an earthquake. British biologist Rupert Sheldrake has submitted a very provocative hypothesis that whenever a member of a species learns something new, the "causative field" or their behavioral blueprint is altered. If the new behavior is repeated enough times, a "morphic resonance" is established that will affect every member of the species.

Intuition has been called a mystical power, a guardian angel that takes care of us. Yet no one knows what it is, except that it is knowledge gained without rational thought and that it comes from some awareness just below the conscious level. In Eastern philosophy, it is believed that each mind has access to the whole of a universal intellectual pattern.

According to Roy Rowan, in his book *The Intuitive Manager,* "New ideas spring from a mind that organizes experiences, facts, and relationships to discern a path that has not been taken before. Somewhere along this uncharted path, intuition compresses years of learning and experience into an instantaneous flash."

In *The Book of Floating*, author Michael Hutchison writes, "In recent years many have recognized the dangers of left-hemisphere dominance and have undertaken various ways to emphasize the right-brain functions. Meditation, yoga, chanting, dancing, running, guided dreaming, visualization, self-hypnosis, and many other techniques have been used to open up the right hemisphere." He personally advocates suspended rest in a flotation tank as the most efficient means of gaining access to your creative and intuitive nature.

There are certain activities or surroundings that can be very conducive to intuition. You'll need to experiment and find out what works best for you. The most important step is for the mind to be receptive to different ideas and to have faith in your own abilities. In the book *Psycho-Cybernetics,* Dr. Maxwell Maltz wrote, "You must learn to trust your creative mechanism to do its work and not jam it by becoming too concerned or too anxious as to whether it will work or not, or by attempting to force it by too much conscious effort. You must let it work, rather than make it work." Trusting yourself is an important part of learning to use intuition.

I am not suggesting with this chapter that you don't do your homework when you make financial or business decisions. It's important to do the research to support your feelings. What I am suggesting is that you also listen to your hunches, then make a decision. Listening to your intuition is just adding another resource to your existing tool box of strategies.

Sanaya Roman, in her book *Personal Power Through Awareness*, wrote, "Intuition talks to you in present time. Through urges, flashes of ideas, insights and feelings, intuition moves you in certain directions. To hear it, pay attention to your inner world of ideas and feelings. If you are forcing yourself to do one thing while your feelings are urging you to do something else, you are not paying attention to your intuition. Your intuition sends you messages constantly, telling you every moment what to do to open your energy. It is always directing you towards aliveness and a higher path."

One of the best tips I can share with you for making a decision about almost anything is *if it feels right*—if things seem to fall into place easily, if people are cooperative, and you have a very positive feeling, it usually means it's a go. However, monitor your feelings; if your decision feels unsure, you feel anxious and nervous, if you experience a certain tightness in your body, then maybe you should postpone your decision till these uneasy feelings go away, or you've gathered more information. It's very important to access your emotions. Keep yourself centered to feel in control and do what you believe in.

The following recommended procedures will help guide your intuition to work for you.

Get into a receptive state, prepare your environment to where you feel comfortable and you can hear yourself think. If you're stressed-out or pressured, you won't have access to your intuition.

1. Have faith that you can tap into your own abilities to use your intuition.
2. Change your daily routines, do things differently. This stimulates creative thoughts.
3. Listen to your body; that is why we call intuition a "gut" feeling. The solar plexus is a large network of nerves located behind the stomach and is said to be the seat of emotion. This allows many of us have an accurate, gut-level reaction to many situations.
4. Allow yourself to redefine the problem frequently; writing out the problem gives you the opportunity to see the problem from a different perspective.
5. Open your mind to consider many alternatives simultaneously—be flexible.
6. Allow yourself to play; you don't have to be sitting in your office to come up with creative and intuitive solutions! Take a walk, feed the birds, play hooky for an hour and then come back to work on the problem.
7. Adopt a childlike view of the situation. Children often see the obvious when we as adults make things much harder than they really need to be.
8. Pay attention to your dreams and your daydreams—they are your personal, non-verbal imagery.
9. Clearly distinguish between real obstacles and imagined ones that don't have to be surmounted.
10. Do not feel you must start at the beginning of a problem; you can think about the problem at any stage to gain insight on it.
11. No one is 100-percent right all the time; give yourself permission not to have instant success.
12. Take action on your insights; start investigating with the approach of "will this hunch logically work?"
13. Build quiet think time into your everyday schedule; learn to meditate. With this quiet time,

start to think metaphorically, in pictures, hunches, or feelings, using your imagination as much as possible.

Meditation or Quiet Time

One of the benefits of meditation is that it helps you achieve a state where you can relax and tune out the outside world. It is only when you are relaxed that you can be creative and listen to your intuition. When you are uptight, anxiety and fearful thoughts will hold you back from listening to those inner urges of what you really want for yourself. Taking time to meditate allows you to align yourself with your highest and best good. Creating a time each day for inner reflection and listening to yourself helps to reduce your stress, allows you to feel centered and in control of your life. One of the greatest benefits of meditation is that it can remove you from the customary state of awareness and allow a new perception to flow into your consciousness. When practiced on a regular basis, meditation can relax and heal your body, making you more efficient mentally, creatively, and intuitively. Meditation also results in a more balanced, integrated, and harmonious personality. By using quiet time we are simply stilling the ordinary, habitual chatter of our minds and relaxing the tensions in our stress-reactive bodies. It's a very simple process.

How to Meditate

1. Create a quiet environment, where you will not be disturbed for twenty minutes or more.
2. Wear loose, comfortable clothes.
3. Quiet the body. You can sit cross-legged or sit in a chair with both feet flat on the floor, or you can lie on a mat/bed or the floor! The spine should be straight but comfortable. The body should be relaxed and at ease so you don't focus on it. You may want to start to quiet the body by doing some relaxation exercise. Try some deep breathing exercises by beginning with deep inhalations, holding your breath for a few

seconds, then completing the cycle with a long slow exhalation.

4. Focus on a constant mental stimulus, such as a phrase, sound, or word repeated silently. You can also fix your gaze on an outer focal point, such as a tree, a stream, a candle, or anything that is pleasing to you. This simply helps you to shift away from your logical, externally-oriented world.

5. Invoke a passive attitude. Don't work hard at meditating; you don't have to achieve anything, you're not in a competition. If distracting thoughts intrude, acknowledge them but let them pass through your mind—your goal is to be receptive. If you are uncomfortable—move, if you have an itch—scratch it, and return to the process.

6. Allow yourself to just be in the quiet of your mind. Feel yourself going into your inner reality. Feel the centering, aligning, and balancing of the real you. (There is an old saying: Praying is talking to God; meditation is listening to God.)

7. After meditation, give yourself a few minutes to write down any thoughts or insights that came to you. Then bring yourself up slowly and gently back into physical reality.

A dear friend of mine told me that she had received more emotionally therapeutic effects from meditation in one year than from all the years of professional counseling she's endured. Meditation allowed her to somehow stand apart from her emotionally hurt and angry self and take on an attitude much like that of a detached observer. She was able to get past the negative past influences and focus on what was good about her life. Her new attitude has allowed her to feel healed, and she now has much better relationships than she could have ever had without taking on a different perspective of her past experiences. She reported to me that meditation is the best way to listen to her intuition, and she never misses an opportunity to spend twenty to thirty minutes a day meditating.

For a number of years, I had been interested in attending the Monroe Institute of Applied Science, on 850 acres known as the New Land, located in the foothills of Virginia's Blue Ridge Mountains. I really didn't know very much about the place other than that the key process employed there is called Hemi-Sync™. This is an acoustical system developed and patented by Robert Monroe, who was once a very successful former radio and television executive and is author of the best-selling books *Journeys Out of the Body* and *Far Journeys.*

One day I called the Monroe Institute and requested information be sent to my office. On the same day that the information arrived, I happened to be talking to the editor of a magazine and I mentioned my interest in going. She said to me, "That's interesting; we just had a meeting and wanted to ask someone to go who would write a story about the experience for our magazine!" Within two weeks, my visit was all arranged with almost no effort on my part. Thousands of people from all walks of life, including professionals from science and academia from all over the world, have visited the institute to participate in brain-study workshops. The workshops implement the new technology of Hemi-Sync™ to create an altered state of awareness by introducing a slightly different sound-wave frequency into each ear. These sound waves build a synchronized resonance between the two hemispheres of the brain. According to the Monroe Institute, sound-wave patterns can be used for relief from pain and drug abuse, insomnia, rapid physical healing, accelerated learning, creativity enhancement, stress reduction, increased concentration, weight loss, gaining confidence, or simply improving your tennis or golf game. These claims were backed up by numerous physicians, educators, engineers, and scientists. Over 200,000 people around the world have experienced Hemi-Sync™ through audio tapes and brain study workshops.

What happened after I arrived literally changed my life. I have been meditating for many years and know in my heart that the most profound answers to my problems in life have always come from my intuition. My inner guidance has always led me to the right resources or the right people who could give me the answers. Robert Monroe says that the programs are aimed at enabling participants to experience profound areas of awareness. This six-day program quite simply allows you to reach meditative states deeper than I had ever had the opportunity to reach before. I spent six days learning from myself about who I was and exactly what I wanted out of my life. I released a lot of old programming and fears that held me back from truly living the way I wanted to live. The strongest example was that I had been working on writing this book for over two years. Deep down I kept sabotaging myself. Everything I wrote, I tore apart; I couldn't feel confident that it was good enough. I kept going in circles; writing and rewriting chapters, changing directions of the book, and in general frustrating myself. In the Monroe Institute's program, I "got" from my intuition or my inner guidance, the information on why I had blocked myself from writing. I saw clearly, for the first time, why I had not allowed myself to write. My guidance told me to simply write what I knew. That was all I could do in life anyway. Just be the best I could be.

When I left the Monroe Institute, I felt more at peace with myself than I ever had in my entire life. I somehow got what my intuition told me and stopped trying to be anything but who I really was. That week was one of the greatest gifts I have ever given myself in my life. It allowed me to accept and love myself right where I am now. When I returned home, I sat down and started writing. My writing pattern usually required about a month or two to write one chapter. I now was writing a chapter a week! I couldn't believe the change that had taken place with my creativity. As I look back, I can see that I didn't develop any more creativity or become a better writer overnight; what really happened was that I released my own brakes, I let myself fly! I believed and had faith that my intuition was telling me the truth. I started living my life on faith that I could be as creative and productive as I wanted to be. The result of this tremendous experience has been that I know all the answers we will ever need can be accessed by listening to our inner voice.

Review Your Past Successes

One way to motivate youself to take the leap of faith and start to listen and act on your intuition is to look back at all the times you've acted on your instincts and were amazed at your success. You were listening to your intuition! Following your intuition requires you to love and have trust in yourself. The payoff for listening to those inner whispers and acting on them can make the difference in how fulfilling your life can be.

I would like to end this chapter with another personal story. After my house was robbed and the insurance company had replaced all my jewelry that was stolen, I became very security-conscious. Since I was away from home a great deal of the time, I started hiding my jewelry.

Every week I would try to outdo myself on finding good hiding places. One week I created such a good place to hide my jewelry that I lost it! For several weeks I looked and looked for my jewelry but with no success. One night at dinner, I was telling a good friend about how I had lost my jewelry when she said to me, "Lee, I cannot believe my ears; you teach this stuff!"

That night, just before I went to sleep, I said to myself, "Self, you know where that jewelry is and I want you to tell me when I wake up." Well, "Self" was being a bit stubborn and I had to do this exercise for several days. One morning at exactly 2:45 A.M., I sat up in bed and my intuition told me to look in my garage, in an old chair that Goodwill was picking up that morning! Thank goodness I listened to myself and checked out that chair for the jewelry, or you can bet I would be down at Goodwill buying back that chair!

CHAPTER
–8–
CAPITALIZING ON CHANGE

"If You Master Yourself, You Can Master Anything"
—Ancient Proverb

Many years have passed since author and scientist C.P. Snow wrote that, until this century, social change was so slow that it would pass unnoticed in one person's lifetime. Change is happening so fast now that it's almost impossible to document. Change is everywhere in every walk of life. The world is getting smaller because of communication and the processing of information. Competition is now stronger than ever in our global economy. Instead of letting change overwhelm us, we must become adaptive. To make the most of change, we must make our own luck by learning new skills and attitudes. Instead of seeing change as something to resist with fear, we have the power within us to see change as a new and wonderful opportunity to tap into our potential.

Old habits, solutions, and experience may not always work in today's fast-paced world. We must make new choices. Our goal in this chapter is to become conscious of how we are using our mental, physical, emotional, and spiritual life energies in dealing with change. Our thoughts, intentions, and actions create our future. It is said that Destiny is the consequence of your daily decisions. It is the decisions you make in your life, not the circumstances, that will make the crucial difference in how you handle the change that is taking place daily.

Dealing with change takes determination, persistence, and

courage. Our challenge is to enlarge the repertoire of resources we have in order to deal with change and prosper from that change. We want to remove our past limitations and create strategies to increase the quality of our lives. It's important that we become conscious of how our actions create effects and how those effects create our future.

It is very empowering to realize that by choosing our response to any circumstance, we powerfully affect our future. By taking responsibility for our own lives, we alter the circumstance and its outcome. The true test of an individual's character is when the events around them are not supportive. Sometimes we have to gracefully accept that there are things we cannot change and learn to live with them, even when we don't like it. In making this powerful choice, we do not allow the problems to control us. The Alcoholics Anonymous program sums it up well with the Prayer of Serenity: "Lord, give me the courage to change the things which can and ought to be changed, the serenity to accept the things which can't be changed, and the wisdom to know the difference."

James Allen, in his famous book *As A Man Thinketh*, says, "Circumstance does not make the man, it reveals him to himself."

The next time you meet with adversity, temporary defeat, or failure, remember that you may have no control over the revolutionary changes or unpleasant circumstances, but you do have control over your reaction to these circumstances. Exercise this privilege by searching for the seed of opportunity, which is carried in every experience of adversity and sorrow.

We must choose to be proactive in life and not let life happen to us. We must be driven by our values and goals, not by outside circumstances. You do not have to be a victim of circumstance; you make your own environment because you are the creator of your life by using your thoughts and actions. Your *greatness comes from within*, so start today to capitalize on your own talents and potential. The emphasis in our lives should be on developing the vision; to see beyond the current situation, we must develop mental control over our emotions, feel our own power, and assume responsibility for our future.

To deal effectively with change, we must question our perceptions. The way we look at the world clearly determines how we interpret the events going on inside and outside of ourselves. Our perceptions filter all our incoming experiences of life. These perceptions are strongly held rules and regulations in our mind that can blind us to creative solutions. When we resist new ideas, we reject new ways of thinking before we've even given them a chance.

We think the past will be the same as the future. Our vision is narrowed by the old way of looking at life; from business people not seeing new opportunities or new markets, to parents not questioning whether their children should be brought up in the same way their parents raised them. We tend to hang on to traditions, ignoring new ways of thinking, because we're not used to looking at our problems from a broader perspective.

I would like to introduce an important concept that you will be reading and hearing more about in the future. It's already a buzzword in business—that buzzword is "paradigm" (pronounced *"pair-a-dime."*) A paradigm is a pattern, model, theory, perception, or frame of reference. In a general sense, it's the way we see the world and the way we perceive and understand or interpret life. The easiest way for us to understand paradigms is to think of them as maps. Keep in mind that the map is not the landscape. It's simply an explanation or model. Generally speaking, it's the way we "see" the world, the way we interpret or understand it.

The term "paradigm shift" was introduced in Thomas Kahn's book *The Structure of Scientific Revolutions*. He demonstrated how almost every significant breakthrough in science is first a break with tradition apart from old ways of thinking, and old paradigms.

By nature, we attempt to discover the future by first looking at our history. In the sixties, our society thought that the ideal family had four children; the mother maintained home and child-rearing while the father worked. Society believed that you would go to work for one company and be taken care of the rest of your life. We believed gas would be cheap forever and products from Japan would always be junk. We laughed at the thought of paying for cable TV.

And we were very wrong. Because we thought our past would determine our future, we missed out on many wonderful and exciting opportunities. Back in the early sixties when *Made in Japan* was labeled on products, people commonly associated those products with phrases like cheap, junk, poor quality, copies, and imitation. Today when those same three words, *Made in Japan,* are affixed to an item, a totally different impression comes to mind—high-tech, expensive, innovative, and high-quality.

The point that I am illustrating here is that there was a paradigm shift. In the early fifties, an American, Ed Deming, went to Japan and helped the Japanese develop and adopt a new set of rules. These rules are now called Japanese management or participative management. But the bottom line is that they've developed something called "Zero Defect Production." Simply put, they created an epidemic of quality. And, according to all the experts that deal with trends of the future, if you don't get it, your business will not survive.

You see, when a paradigm shifts, we all go back to the beginning. No matter how successful you were in your market share, suddenly everyone is equal again. This is why I believe there will be available in the future opportunities of which we have not yet even dreamed. There are more scientists alive today than at any other time in history, and technology is changing so fast that we can hardly keep up with it. This all means that, with the right attitude and an eye for opportunities, you can use to your advantage the paradigm shifts that will occur in our future.

Here is another famous example of a paradigm shift. The Swiss had dominated the world in watchmaking for over 100 years by 1968. They had more than 65 percent of the world market share and 80 percent of the profits— complete market domination. However, by 1978, to the

Swiss' horror and disbelief, their market share shriveled to less than 10 percent. Over the next three years they had to release more than 75 percent of their 65,000 watchmakers.

This came about with the Swiss invention of the quartz-movement watch. The inventors presented it to their manufacturers in 1967; but the manufacturers were confident that the general public wouldn't buy it because it didn't have the usual gears that everyone was accustomed to having in their watches. The manufacturers were so convinced of its lack of potential that they did not have it patented. The inventors were still proud of their watch, and they displayed it at the annual watch congress in 1968. Representatives from Texas Instruments of America and Sony of Japan stopped by their booth and the rest is watchmaking history.

The invention of the quartz-movement watch initiated a paradigm shift where everyone in the market went back to zero. The Swiss were blinded by the success of their old paradigm; the new watch did not fit into the rules they were used to. Today Japan is the leading watchmaker of the world, when in 1968 they had no market share at all. Now the Swiss are regaining on their old success with the invention and effective marketing of the Swatch watch.

From this example you can see that your past successes do not equal guaranteed success in the future. Your past successes can in fact blind and influence your perceptions of the future. Let's look at some of the reasons we resist change and blind ourselves from opportunities and new solutions in the future.

Reasons We Resist Change

Old Habits. We are all creatures of habit. Of course a habit is a way of doing something we have comfortably taken for granted. It could mean habits such as overeating, smoking, or the way we drive or prepare a meal. Since our habits and patterns of behavior have been reinforced by our parents, teachers, workplace, and our society, it is very difficult to change, even if we don't like the way things are. These habits are familiar, easy, and routine. Whereas the new way, the change, is a disruption to our life's routine. We tell ourselves that it just takes too much effort to change. Think of all the broken New Year's resolutions. We have the same problems at work; we become ingrained in the procedures. When it's time to change, we find it an inconvenience—that takes too much energy.

It is important to understand that our mental and emotional attitudes are shaped by our habits. If we welcome change, we look forward to experimentation and challenges. However, if we're in a rut and don't like to experiment with anything new, we shut down any real opportunities for growth and new solutions.

Our culture also affects our ability to change. If there is strong peer pressure to stick to status quo, what's always been accepted as standard, it becomes very hard for any individual to change or act differently. The sheer force of our habits hinders our vision of new opportunities and that's why we resist change.

Insecurity. Personal insecurity is another reason we resist change. We all fear something. We all fear that our lives or our jobs will not be as good in the future as they are now. Some of us fear we will be worse off because of less money, fewer resources, a loss of the creature comforts we have become accustomed to; we fear fewer opportunities for advancement or loss of respect. All these fears and feelings of uncertainty create anxiety and stress. In reality, the anticipation of a negative event is much worse than the reality of change.

Typical Insecurities We Associate With Change

Fear of Failure. We tend to resist change because, at that moment in time, we feel confident of our abilities to cope and perform well in our position. When we have to adjust to new environments, learn new skills, and/or work with new people, we often fear we will not adjust well and will ultimately fail. Because of our fear of the unknown, we resist change of any kind.

Fear of Looking Incompetent. New technology is changing our lives in the way we work and live daily. We often fear we will look foolish and stupid during the learning process. We feel easily intimidated by those who seem to be more technically minded. Many times we refuse to learn about the new phone system or computer simply because we feel inadequate.

Fear of the Unknown. Our feelings of insecurity increase when we don't know all that is going on. In many companies, Management has been very tight-lipped about providing information at just the right time for the people involved. Questions we want and have the right to know are: What changes are taking place? Where will this lead? How does this affect me? What responsibilities am I expected to take on? What new skills must I learn?

Misinformation. When there is a lack of information, speculation spawns negative rumors. Rumors, in turn, can create even more fear and stress. In reality, people can deal with whatever is happening as long as they are given the truth.

Learned Helplessness. Learned Helplessness is giving in to being a victim and reactor to life; we look for reasons why things won't work out for us. What you focus on becomes your reality—when you focus on why you cannot succeed in any given endeavor, you supply yourself with the reason not to try. Because of old programming, some people just quit as if they had learned that it was not possible to do more because they are frightened by the world they find themselves in. As in fairy tales, we sometimes expect someone to save us and take care of us; we often fall back into the child-like mentality that our parents, spouses, bosses, or government will bail us out.

Strategies For Dealing With Change

First, you must accept the idea that YOU MUST CHANGE to adapt to new markets, new environments, new technology, new people, and new circumstances.

Second, you must believe you have the ability to change and take 100 percent responsibility for it.

Third, you have to BELIEVE you can change. A belief is simply that feeling of certainty about what something means.

Fourth and finally, you must always be looking for the benefits of change and how you can capitalize on the change.

Anticipate and Expect Change
To Be a Permanent Part of Your Life

The one constant in life *is* Change; it is the tool of human progress because it gives us new opportunities. Francis Bacon once said, "Man will make more opportunities than he finds." Start today to think of yourself as a trend spotter. This enables you to look past your current needs and see the "big picture." Ask yourself, "What is the next step in my life?" If you work for a company, ask yourself, "Where is the company and my position headed?" What are your options? What is the worst thing that could happen? What would be your strategy if the worst did happen? Anticipate and plan for it—but don't dwell on it.

According to Emily Kolnow, co-author of *Congratulations! You've Been Fired*, "You should plan on being fired, because there is no such thing as job security. Taking steps toward a new career should be part of your everyday work life." Job advisers agree; the ultimate career crime is failing to build a bridge to your next position by looking ahead and expecting change. An important strategy is to have your antennae up, posturing yourself to make a move if the opportunity comes along that is right for you. It used to be considered disloyal to your company to seek out other opportunities, but, first and foremost, you must be loyal to yourself.

How does the human spirit thrive or even survive in the chaos that we experience daily? According to Jacquelyn Wonder and Priscilla Donovan, authors of *Whole Brain Thinking and the Flexibility Factor,* the answer lies in flexibility, the ability to bend without breaking. Flexibility makes it possible to respond to change, adapting to make modifications and variations. They state in their book that change always brings out our creativity, whether through hardship, adaptation, or developing something new. In every change there is opportunity for growth and excitement. That is what success is about—seeing opportunity and capitalizing on it. One of your greatest sources of power is your ability to be flexible. When you stubbornly hold on to old ideas of the way things should be, you shut yourself off from new solutions.

Cheryl Rich Heisler, president of a consulting firm that helps executives explore career options, says, "If you peg yourself as a a one-track professional, you have the potential to be very unhappy. Instead of thinking, I am a public-relations professional and always will be, think of yourself as a communications professional, one who could do other jobs in the communications field."

Bob Hope's various talents and flexible attitude enabled him to be successful in one of the world's toughest businesses for over fifty years. He had the ability to recognize change and then capitalize on it using his unique talents. He started out in vaudeville, moved on to Broadway, then movies, radio, and finally television, mastering each medium along the way. He had what I call the skill of awareness. He was able to recognize the changes taking place around him. He saw clearly how the industry was changing and tailored his style of performing accordingly. Bob Hope's ability to change with the times and capitalize on changes around him made him one of the wealthiest men in show business!

Be An Optimist

Success in life is 80 percent Attitude and 20 percent Aptitude. We can learn anything we are willing to spend the time and energy to learn. It's our attitude that will make a difference if we are open to change and able to use change to empower us and our future. Robert Schuller said, "Success doesn't come the way you think it does—it comes from the way you think." Oliver Wendell Holmes said, "What lies behind us and what lies before us are tiny matters compared to what lies within us." Quite simply, you have more leverage for success when you expect to win.

You get in life what you focus on. If you dwell on limitations, you will reach them. You will have a better life in every way if you make the least of the worst while making the most of the best.

One attribute that separates the average from the out-standing is the willingness to look for the positive angle in all situations. Optimists know that many times difficult situations or adversity will bring out hidden resources and capabilities. They have made an internal decision to excel, to rise to the occasion. Optimists choose to see opportunities where others choose to see problems. Thomas Edison said, "If we did all the things in life we were capable of doing we would literally astound ourselves." Another quote I enjoy is "Real difficulties can be overcome, it is only the imaginary ones that are unconquerable." Update your perceptions of what is really going on around you. How can you *make these changes work for you* instead of against you?

See Yourself As Self-Employed

A huge mistake in life is to think you are working for someone else. You are working for yourself no matter what your job title. If you think of yourself as self-employed, you never put your destiny in someone else's hands. Empower yourself today while you have the resources to create a workable strategy that guarantees survival and prosperity for the next decade. Observe the trends around you and alter your course to capitalize on them. This allows you to get a sense of the future and act on it—instead of merely reacting to the present circumstances. Giving yourself permission to create a new label for youself as self-employed will program your brain to stay tuned into what is going on around you. Understanding that you are 100-percent responsible for the outcomes in your life gives you the motivation to try new strategies and approaches that will utilize the resources you already have.

If you are having a hard time right now doing your best for your boss, do it for yourself! Do the type of work you'd do if you were an independent contractor—if you were the boss! Your attitude and work will improve, which in turn will help you receive good recommendations from your present employer should you ever decide to go to another company or begin one for yourself.

Become A Peak Performer

Recently, I interviewed a true peak performer who happened to be a supervisor in a manufacturing plant. She had become bored with her job and decided to look for another job. After three months of searching, she realized that it wasn't the job that was the problem; it was her attitude. She decided a shift in routine and focus would rekindle her enthusiasm for the position. She began to look at her position as more than just the supervisor of other people. Her new goal was to learn at least three ways each week to improve the work of the plant and her performance with her work crew. She not only improved her own attitude and outlook of her position, but, in turn, inspired her work crew. And the department improved their productivity by more than 25 percent in a single three-month period!

To become a peak performer, you must consciously and persistently develop the characteristics that allow you to be flexible, teachable, and "big picture" oriented. You must be willing to venture out of your comfort zone where things are unchallengingly familiar and be willing to take calculated risks. You have the ability to become a peak performer in whatever you do. You must learn to tap into the abilities, talents, and skills we all have, to take care of yourself. Most importantly, you must be willing to do what it takes to put your skills into action. Peak performers are also realists who believe that, in the final analysis, they will make it and will overcome any barriers, achieving positive results. As Robert Schuller said, "Tough times never last— tough people do."

Be A Visionary

To capitalize on change you must see the "big picture." Every job you've ever had, every experience, book, and class has helped educate you for exactly where you are at this point in time. The same process will hold true in the future. See every opportunity to experience life as just that—experience. Sometimes it comes as the result of poor judgment. Some have even said that experience is what you get when you don't get what you want! What's important here is to focus on what you have learned; look back at your mistakes and failures and see how they gave you the resources and insights you needed today. We all go to the famous school of hard knocks to climb the ladders of success; whether it's to become a manager or a better parent, you must gain a certain amount of experience to get there.

Be A Student Of New Skills and Knowledge

Not so very long ago, the general population thought that once you had completed college or trade school you were done with learning. Today, if you see people with the attitude that they are already educated and they rely on their past skills and knowledge, you will not be seeing them much longer. They will lose their careers to intense global competition and new technology. People who expect to keep up today must expose themselves to lifelong learning.

There's no such thing as job security, but you can have employment security by developing a wide range of skills through job-sponsored opportunities and other career-related channels. The more you learn, the more valuable you'll be to current or future employers. Scott DeGarmo, editor of *Success* magazine, said, "The strength of an individual is based on his possessing a scarce resource; general knowledge that can be quickly adapted to new circumstances. Education must be an ongoing process with much acquired via journalistic sources."

An important point to consider is this: if you box yourself into a company with just one career or one vision, what happens to you if that company perishes? The same concept applies to relationships; if you depend on another person to take care of you and support you, what happens if suddenly that support system is no longer there?

Victims learn too late. It is never wise to depend on the company, the boss, or another person to take care of you. According to Charles Garfield, author of the book *Peak Performers*, "People now must expect to learn new jobs, two or three times in their lives." This is because change is happening so fast that our past skills and knowledge can no longer support us for a lifetime. If we do not learn new skills, we have no way of achieving upward mobility or any personal security.

Our real source of wealth in life is the information, knowledge, and energy we have inside of us for taking action. We must make new choices by learning, training, experimentation, and integration of new information.

When you have a clear and compelling view of the benefits of learning, you will strongly influence your own future and the attitudes of the people around you. New training will open up your mind to creative ways to enhance your life and prosperity. Think of your mind as a parachute; it works only when opened!

Check out how other successful people fit learning new skills into their already over-budgeted life.

One option used by all successful peak performers is utilizing "dead time." On an average week you spend over seven hours commuting to and from work and taking care of personal errands. Why not invest in audio learning cassette tapes? When I use the word "invest," I mean just that. The few dollars you invest in learning the many skills you need to get ahead in today's world will give you an edge in the ability to see new opportunities.

There are so many subjects available to learn about: time and stress management, negotiation skills, leadership and management, relationships, and even parenting skills that would give you new options and new choices. Today's opportunities for growth and expansion through self-education are incredibly varied. There are hundreds of professional seminars, corporate in-house training workshops, college extension courses, video and audio learning cassettes, and a multitude of resourceful books for you to choose from. It's important that you take advantage of these resources if you want to be successful—don't try to reinvent the wheel. The new knowledge you gain now will make the difference in your future, from your advancement potential to the way you cope daily with your life and family.

Adult learning has been revolutionized like almost everything else in life. Even if you hated being a student before, you now have the power to choose what you're interested in and wish to learn. This new type of mind-set will result in an entirely new set of values and resources. Everything you learn can be used in some way—all of your skills are transferable. When you change your view of who you are and what you are capable of learning, you change your destiny. You are no longer merely reacting to the present; you are creating your future by anticipating your learning needs. Adapting your skills to those needs and taking action by following through with this type of behavior gives you the power to deal with whatever changes you encounter.

Change Your Self-Talk

Be aware of the directions you give your brain. Your internal dialogue is how you create your emotions. Negative self-talk messages will cause you to give up before you even try something new. For example: "I can't do this; I don't understand; I'm not good at technical tasks; I'll look stupid; What's the point, as soon as I learn it they will change it; Why should I care, they don't; I'm too old to learn new skills; If only. . .; They make me feel stupid; That's just the way I am; There's nothing I can do."

How many of those have you used? Change your self-talk to be positive reinforcement for your computer. A focused mind creates emotional calm and peace—a positive outlook creates more options for creative solutions. Use instead: "If they can do it, so can I; I'll never know until I give it a try; I've succeeded before during difficult challenges and I know I can succeed again; It's great learning new skills, it gives me more experience and resources; So what if it won't be easy—I still want to give it my best shot; Let's look at our alternatives; I can choose a new approach; I choose. . .I prefer. . .I will. . ."

Change Creates Excellence

One of the first steps to creating excellence in your life is to remove mediocrity in your environment, habits, attitudes, and behavior. List the things around you that cause you to act average. These are the things that render you powerless to go beyond the limits you have arbitrarily set for yourself. Commitment to excellence is the product of consistently going beyond your limits.

Homework Assignment

1. Beginning today, accept change as normal.
2. Surround yourself with individuals who ask more of you than you do yourself.
3. Always remain open and receptive to new ideas, options, and solutions.
4. Give yourself permission to see yourself as continually in the process of becoming.

I would like to leave you with the empowering thought that it's to your benefit to begin to develop an attraction for change. By doing this you no longer have to waste your life energy being upset or wishing things were different. Developing an attraction for change will also help you not jump to conclusions or hold on to fixed opinions without researching your options. The more we honor our own power to deal with life, the less we will feel cheated or stressed out by change.

The more we open our minds to investigate the new opportunities, the more positive aspects will become obvious because of change. We must allow ourselves to see change as a rewarding challenge and not as a threat. The truth is that profiting from change takes excellence, hard work, a strong mental attitude, and yes—it will take courage. It should—because that is what true success is all about!

_9_

DEVELOPING THE
ENTREPRENEURIAL SPIRIT

Harvey Mackay said in his book *Swim with the Sharks,* "Capitalism constantly devours its own creations and gives birth to new ones." He went on to say that no matter how safe a little niche you may have thought you have found for yourself, in a world where capitalism constantly destroys its own creations, your jobs will change, as will the skills needed to perform them.

It seems that everything we have traditionally taken for granted and relied on for survival can no longer be trusted. We must toss out the old concepts we associated with the meaning of success. I believe the problem is not so much the changing world, but our perception of it. Rather than be overwhelmed by random change, we can choose to see this time as one of opportunity. This is the time to stop living the old, dated traditions passed down from generation to generation and create an entirely new paradigm for success.

Life in today's world holds an infinite number of possibilities for each of us to apply our talents in ways of which we may have never before dreamed. Why? In the words of Ralph Waldo Emerson, "Every adversity, every unpleasant circumstance and every failure carries within it the seed of an equivalent benefit." When survival is paramount, we no longer have the luxury of mediocrity. Crisis forces us to step outside our limitations—to look deeper and tap new resources and new talents to deal with reality.

Our past programming hasn't prepared us to live in this new fast-paced reality. In the past, our world has asked for conformity but creation demands change. The old saying, "If you do everything the way you've always done it, you'll get what you've always gotten," is no longer true. To be successful today, we need to change the ground rules from old traditions that are no longer working to create a new repertoire of skills, strategies, and resources that will allow us to deal more effectively with the world we now live in.

I firmly believe that, to be truly happy in life, you must capitalize on your talents and the circumstances surrounding you. It just makes good common sense to take advantage of what you were born with. One of the talents with which you were born is called survival. If you polish that talent it can also be called Entrepreneurialism. A way to capitalize on your talents is to give yourself a new label—begin to think of yourself as an entrepreneur. In the dictionary, the definition of an entrepreneur is a person who organizes and manages an enterprise or business with considerable initiative—one who undertakes some task.

Throughout my life I've used this talent to determine my needs and then satisfy each need as an avenue for creating money and success. Since I didn't have the traditional education to prepare me for any type of specific career, I was forced to sharpen an attitude of self-reliance that I believe, in the next decade, will be one of the most necessary skills to develop.

The purpose of this chapter is to share with you some hard-hitting, winning strategies aimed at helping you to once again create passion and excitement in your life. You will learn to do this by tapping your own unique talents and capitalizing on them to make your dreams come true. This chapter will stimulate you to adopt an "entrepreneurial" style of thinking that will allow you to chart a course in uncharted territory, teaching you to depend on inner resources rather than outer ones.

Incorporate Yourself

Your strategy must be to become the president of a corporation called "Your Life." You are to incorporate yourself mentally and begin thinking of yourself as a company with one employee. It's important to remember that using this mental strategy doesn't mean that you are any less loyal to your present employer. What it does mean, however, is that you keep your long-term interests for yourself and your family at the forefront of your thinking. Your career and personal growth depend on your mind-set of being 100-percent responsible for your own life.

Today, security must flow from the individual—not the job. Your biggest resource for the future must be the ability to take your current knowledge and adapt it to new circumstances. You must develop sharp antennae, constantly scanning the landscape of your life for new opportunities. Be willing to take new risks by changing your strategies and future goals; open your mind to learn new information to deal with the ever-changing environment.

In the past, the decision to pursue the entrepreneurial life style was the by-product of dissatisfaction with the job, frustration with the boss, or the sudden loss of employment. These days, with people being squeezed out of their jobs because of down-sizing, merging, and businesses simply going under, it's clear that we have to look to our future with a new perspective. We can no longer hope to go to work for one company and expect to be taken care of the rest of our lives. We are being forced to become more resourceful and flexible when earning a living.

I believe that, in our current and future environment, the most important rule to remember is that the rules are always changing and you must learn to adapt to these new circumstances. It's easier to adapt when you acknowledge yourself as an entrepreneur. If you are currently working for a company, I'm not suggesting that you quit to become self-employed. What I am suggesting is—that to create security for yourself—you develop what I call the entrepreneurial spirit.

This spirit empowers you to seize opportunities and cut your losses when necessary and, in general, allows you to see more options available to you in life. You have to give yourself permission to see yourself with a new label to encourage the abilities, talents, and potential you have within you to emerge. To have the edge today, it doesn't make any difference if you are self-employed or work for someone else, as long as you have the mind-set of being self-employed.

A wonderful example of the entrepreneurial mind-set while working for a company came from a woman named Anne. She lived in a small town in Maine and had taken my advice about creating her own future. Anne told me she'd been painfully aware that her company, which built pleasure boats, was going through some rough times, as she'd been denied both a raise and promotion for the last two years. She felt that, since she lived in a small town, there wasn't much opportunity to find another job; and, in truth, she really did love the people she had worked with for more than ten years.

Anne listened to my audio learning program "Coping With Change, Life Strategies for the 90s," which inspired her to start looking for some way that she could make more money yet remain with her present company. She explained that one day, while she was in the company's supply room, she noticed how employees just walked in and took whatever they wanted, no questions asked. A light bulb went off in her head casting light on the idea that, if she could find a way to save her employer money, then she might benefit from those savings.

After a few weeks of research, she submitted a proposal to the owner of the company stating that, if she became the office manager, she could save the company $12,000 dollars per year. She requested a $6,000 raise and the new position. She also guaranteed that not only would the company benefit from a sorely-needed office manager, but they would be saving $6,000 per year. The owner of the company was very excited about her proposal but shook his head saying, "We've done everything we can think of to save money; how do you think you can save us $12,000 per year? If you can, you have the job and the raise!!" Anne said she handed over to the company's owner a detailed report recommending that if the supply office were locked and everyone made to fill out requisition forms, there would be less demand for many of the office supplies that seemed to disappear daily. She also had additional suggestions that would save time and thus more money. She got the job and told me that over the last year she actually saved the company a total of $18,000, and they gave her another raise. She added that she has never been happier in her working life. She feels that she created a job that is challenging and personally rewarding.

This is a true life story of how we sometimes can't see the forest for the trees—a company trying to save money, overlooking some very obvious answers. Anne wanted to empower herself and empower her company. A win-win situation and what I call entrepreneurial thinking.

Entrepreneurs are called many things: hardworkers, pioneers, visionaries, and trail blazers. They are the people who are the producers, risk takers, and problem solvers. They have the ability to look ahead, to create, and they have a burning desire to manifest their ideas into the real world. They are not content to just imagine the future; they want to help create it. There are a number of identifying characteristics that will allow you to create this edge and guarantee prosperity for your future.

A Burning Desire To Develop Your Potential

In other words, you have a high need for achievement. Successful entrepreneurs create support for themselves by believing in themselves and their missions or goals. Recent research shows that the need for achievement is higher among successful entrepreneurs than in the average person. Many of the true entrepreneurs I know value using their true potential over approval, recognition, power, prestige, and yes, even money.

Now let's get specific. What does the need to achieve mean? It doesn't necessarily mean that a person has to be a straight-A student, graduate from an Ivy League school, drive the best car, or live in the most expensive neighborhood. Achievement means that you, as an individual, take personal pride in whatever you do, and that you are willing to do whatever it takes to finish whatever you start. You are willing to work long hours, get your hands dirty; you believe that no job is too small and are willing to satisfy the part of yourself that gives you a sense of accomplishment.

High Energy

A high level of energy is another characteristic of a truly successful entrepreneur. In the past, successful entrepreneurs have many times been described as workaholics. I believe being a workaholic today does not benefit you or anyone else. Balance is the key to success. However, most people who truly love what they do would not describe their work as work—after all they love it!

There is a quote I really love from Robert Frost. He commented that "The reason worry kills more people than work, is that more people worry than work." Many times opportunities are disguised as hard work, so most people don't recognize them. But entrepreneurs thrive on identifying opportunities as they arise. They are willing to work hard and create whatever they envision for themselves. They understand you have to earn your way in life.

The Need For Independence

A powerful characteristic that often drives people to become entrepreneurs is a high need for independence. Entrepreneurs are extremely self-reliant. They take the initiative, are decisive, and have a high degree of self-confidence because they believe in themselves and know they can succeed no matter what happens in the outside world. Entrepreneurial success, like any type of success, comes from decisiveness. It's sad that we are not taught how to make successful decisions in our educational system; inevitably most people go through life making decisions by default. They become reactors to options dictated by others or by evolving circumstances. In today's world we must lose the mental and emotional baggage that keeps our decision-making from being more assertive, proactive, and creative. We create our own reality every day with our thoughts, choices, and actions. If you are to succeed in the future with the entrepreneurial spirit, you must break free of your old reactive mode of thinking and switch to a more assertive, proactive mode of behavior. You have to rid yourself of the idea of limited choices. If there is a will, there is always a way!

Good Judgment

To maximize the entrepreneurial spirit you must have good judgment. Almost any successful person, when asked, has said that judgment is almost more important than creativity. They don't feel that they have to invent things, but they do have to recognize a concept and then run with it. They can sense a need for a product or service and are able to focus on filling the need for that product or service.

According to marketing expert Dan Kennedy, in his book *The Ultimate No B.S., No Holds Barred, Kick Butt, Take No Prisoners, and Make Tons of Money Business Success Book*, "You certainly don't need a revolutionary new mousetrap to get rich, there are still plenty of unexploited opportunities in already-established, proven fields of business, and you can build wealth in any number of these fields just by doing things a hair better than the average."

Questions—The Secret Of Success

One of the ways to tap into the Entrepreneurial Spirit to empower yourself with new ideas is simply ask yourself questions. Bob Berkowitz is a friend of mine and has his own television show on the national cable network, CNBC. He once told me an interesting story about the time he was persistent enough to question his own subconscious mind to get the answers he needed, when he was unsure of what he wanted to do with his life.

Bob said that his father, a psyche analyst, told him about a very powerful technique to uncover what you really want to do with your life. He instructed Bob to repeat to himself, before going to sleep at night, something like this: *There is a great idea rattling around my subconscious mind and I now want that great idea to come to my conscious mind.* He related how he had been saying this to himself for several weeks when one day it hit him. No one in the media was specializing in stories and features from the man's point of view. He called up a friend on the *Today* show and the next thing he knew he was doing a regular feature called Today's Man. He began doing research and ended up writing a very successful book called *What Men Won't Tell You But Women Need To Know.* He is now a regular guest on top national talk shows as a recognized expert for men's views. This career path helped him become a successful author and create his own television show, *Up Close & Personal* on CNBC.

I am a firm believer in asking myself questions whenever I need answers or information to aid me in solving a problem or creating more income. I consistently ask myself empowering questions that start my creative abilities working for me, keeping an open mind to spot the answers from many different avenues. Sometimes I'll be listening to a song on the radio or hear a talk show and realize the answer. Often when I'm in need of a solution, I'll pick up a book and skim through it, reading bits and pieces. I hardly ever fail to find creative solutions or thoughts to my problems. Throughout my day, I consistently ask my mind to give me answers. This way I am focusing my attention on looking for an answer, not focusing on the problem. I know in my heart that if I have a problem, then I will find an answer. It's simply a matter of believing in myself enough to know that I have the ability, intelligence, and persistence to find the answer. I refuse to let any problem best me.

Leadership

Another characteristic of successful entrepreneurs is that they see themselves as leaders. There is a difference between managing and leading. As H. Ross Perot said, "People cannot be managed—inventories are managed, people must be led." The truth is that the only person you can manage in this lifetime is yourself. We have to take the responsibility that we are influencing the people around us. Not only our children, spouses and loved ones, but also the people we work with and create services for. It's important to understand the mind-set of seeing yourself as a leader.

Leaders don't expect others to fix the problems of the world. They know they have to contribute in order to see things change for the better. If you examine many of North America's top corporate executives, you will see they fit the entrepreneurial profile. In fact, it's a myth to think that being an entrepreneur is not compatible with big business. Entrepreneurs are people developers—they know how to develop and encourage their own employees and lead a team. When you think of yourself as a leader, you understand the impact that your actions have on others. You are leading by example.

In my seminars I always ask, "How many of you have children?" In response people raise their hands; then I ask, "How many of you have noticed that your children do not always do what you tell them to do?" They all laugh and raise their hands again. Then I say, "Have you noticed they might not do what you tell them to do, but they emulate you?" In reality, our children may not always listen to us, but they will adopt our habits, fears, and beliefs.

Ask yourself daily: What message am I sending out to the world? What environment am I creating? What example am I setting? What do I want to accomplish with my energy today?

A Good Sense of Intuition

To really have your finger on the pulse of what is going on and be able to tap into opportunities available to you, you must start listening to and trusting your intuition. As discussed in Chapter 7, intuition is clearly one of the most important abilities we need to strengthen to enable ourselves to capitalize on changes in the future. Since entrepreneurs have a spirit of adventure, a strong sense of self-reliance, and the willingness to try new things, you too will have to be able to listen to that inner voice for guidance about taking risks and trying new ventures.

Famous minds such as Edison and Einstein believed unquestionably in their intuition. It has been written that, whenever either of them was stymied while trying to create something new, he would first look at the problem from all sides to logically analyze some of the possible solutions. If using just his logical mind and past experience did not solve the problem, he would try to tap into the power of the subconscious mind. He would deliberately take a nap so his conscious mind would rest and the answer could be obtained from his subconscious mind. If a nap was not possible, he would simply stop working on that project and do something entirely different to allow his subconscious mind to search its memory banks to look for possible solutions.

Entrepreneurs Take Time To Think

If you are going to be successful in anything in life, from running a business to raising healthy, happy children, you must make time to be alone and think. Most of us go through life reacting to outside circumstances and rarely have time to just be alone and think. One of the greatest strategies you can use each day is think time. In our culture, we're not experienced with just being alone and quiet and thinking. It seems everywhere you go there is a television on or radio playing. It's as if people are afraid to hear their own thoughts!

You need to take twenty to thirty minutes per day and be where you will not be disturbed—away from telephones, children, and all other distractions. Then simply write out whatever problems you have or the solutions you want on a piece of paper, so you can clearly identify where you want your brain to focus. This way it can immediately start to search for alternative solutions. You will start to see solutions that perhaps were always there but you never considered them before. You will be amazed at how fast you'll realize new perspectives on old problems.

I have learned that one of the best things I can do for my life is to try to combine success habits. I used to run until I heard there was only a twelve-calorie difference between walking briskly and running—so now my favorite exercise is walking! I use my exercise time as my "Think Time." Since I don't want to stop and write down my thoughts nor do I trust my mind to remember my gems of thought, I carry a small tape recorder with me that I use to simply record my thoughts while I walk. I must admit I've come up with some of my best speaking material and problem solving during this time. Just allowing myself to walk in nature and present my mind with clear questions has benefited me greatly in solving my toughest challenges.

Stress experts say that movement promotes creativity; being away from my home or office environment, in a place where I'm not faced with things to be done, allows my mind to free-flow with possible solutions. Not only has the walking reduced my stress and anxiety, it has allowed badly needed think-time that adds great insight into whatever project I'm working on at the moment. I also use this technique whenever I feel upset and unable to make a decision—it relaxes me until I can think clearly and not make rash decisions.

Keep track of your thoughts. Please do not be one of those people who believes, "Well, I thought of it so it can't possibly be any good." That kind of self-talk will smother all your creative thoughts and solutions.

If you study the people who have created great wealth, many will tell you that it was not their learned book knowledge that created their wealth, but their sense of perspective and actions taken on their gut feelings. That inner voice saying "Maybe I should run with this new idea," or "Maybe I shouldn't go with this venture." They took the time not only to think about how to solve their problems, but to speculate on how to make money and success.

Problem Solving

Another great strategy for problem solving and tapping into creative solutions requires just three sheets of paper. On the first, outline the problem precisely and in as much detail as possible. On the second page, write down your feelings about the problem, such as: *I am having anxiety or I am feeling frustrated and worried.* It is important to vent your limiting thoughts and emotions so you can then focus your creative energy on workable solutions.

On the third sheet of paper be as creative and adventuresome as possible on how to solve the problem or achieve the goal. No matter how crazy, outrageous, or ridiculous, write your thoughts down. The power of this exercise is that it to allows you to become more creative in your thinking process and permits you to see the problem from a broader perspective. The first few times you use this method, you may not get all the resourceful answers you want or need. But, like learning a new sport, the more you practice it, the better you will become. If possible, try to avoid writing down the same solutions over and over. We are simply encouraging the mind to look for new possibilities.

Cut Your Losses

Entrepreneurial thinkers are not enslaved by circumstances or negative situations. If they run into a dead end, they simply learn from the experience, cut their losses, and *move on*. This doesn't mean they give up—it simply means they try something new, retaining more experience and knowledge.

Integrity

Another characteristic that really separates the successful entrepreneur's personality from others is personal integrity. This is probably one of the most important characteristics you must have. Your reputation will make or break you. Personal integrity means that you will conduct your business in a way so that you are concerned not only about the outcome for yourself, but also about the outcome for others. You keep your word.

Trend forecaster Faith Popcorn said in a television interview about future trends, "Our whole idea of heroics is changing. And the Good Guy is back. We're going beyond knighting the richest, the cutest, the most powerful, and the sexiest. We are now saluting the Ethical man and woman who make it their business both literally and figuratively to make the world a better place." She went on to say that the nineties is our first truly socially responsible decade. The Decency Decade—dedicated to the three critical E's, Environment, Education, and Ethics.

Entrepreneurs Are Lifetime Learners

Oliver Wendell Holmes, a famous writer, once said, "Man's mind, once stretched by a new concept, never regains its original dimension." True entrepreneurs make a special effort to develop the skill of awareness and absorb what is going on around them. They don't believe they have to reinvent the wheel. They're always looking at what strategies other people are using, for ideas to improve themselves and their world. Everywhere they go they look at what's working and how they can make those concepts work in their businesses, departments, or on particular projects. They observe, adapt, and take action.

It is said that in North America, after formal education, the average person reads only one book a year—I hear it's a sexy novel! Entrepreneurs read everything they can get their hands on that will empower them to be more successful. They use all their dead time, reading whenever waiting for appointments or traveling. Instead of wasting their precious mind time watching mindless television, they read materials that will advance them toward their goal, whether it's to be a better parent, improve a relationship, be a better boss, enhance their personality or have upward mobility. People who want to get ahead invest in themselves. They invest in books, audio and video learning tapes, and seminars to empower them to take advantage of whatever opportunities they can capitalize on.

Entrepreneurs are lifetime learners, curious, open-minded, and—most important of all—receptive to change. They belong to professional organizations where they can meet other people who are idea generators. The old saying "like attracts like" is true—you must deliberately associate with other entrepreneurial-minded people.

Persistence

Persistence is an essential factor in transforming desire into reality. If you study the lives of great artists, you will see that they are unmercifully driven to perfection in their art. But it is the empowering qualities of desire and determination combined with great persistence that will assure attainment of your objectives.

I remember reading where the head of a creative writing department of a university said that he could gauge a student's talent not by the first draft, be it a poem or novel, but by the quality of the tenth draft. Most people become frustrated at having to do things over and over again to improve themselves. But it's only by doing things repetitively that you can perfect your craft.

Alexander Graham Bell once said this about persistence: "What this power is I cannot say. All I know is that it exists and becomes available only when a man is in that state of mind in which he knows exactly what he wants and is fully determined not to quit until he finds it." John D. Rockefeller said, "I do not think there is any other quality so essential to success of any kind as the quality of persistence, it overcomes almost everything, even nature." Likewise, I believe persistence is the ability to keep moving forward, even when you don't see immediate positive results. It's the internal commitment to withstand setbacks again and again without giving up.

There is no question that being an entrepreneur means you must have great desire, clearly defined goals, high motivation, total commitment, and unflagging perseverance. I believe the real motivating force driving successful entrepreneurs is the desire for excellence. Successful entrepreneurs develop that inner part of themselves and take the time to acquire whatever skills are needed for psychological and spiritual growth. They are willing to undertake whatever educational processes will give them the edge to succeed in the future. The underlying theme in their lives is that choice, not chance, determines their destinies and they have the power to be the master of their own fate.

We must constantly challenge ourselves to utilize more of the great potential that is within us. It also takes a tremendous amount of courage to go beyond what we comfortably know and expand our boundaries to claim for ourselves new territories of the mind and spirit. It takes discipline and great perseverance to overcome the fears and doubts that hold us back from really living—but it can be done. If you are willing to give yourself permission to see yourself in a new light and if you are willing to work with yourself, you can acquire the skills needed to transform your life, to start to think and act like an entrepreneur. You can create security for your future simply by changing your thought patterns to explore the great possibilities of life.

As Robert Lewis Stevenson once said, "To be what we are and to become what we are capable of becoming is the only end of life." And from the sports arena, where excellence can be more easily measured, comes a quote from a famous football coach, Vince Lombardi, who said, "The quality of a person's life is in direct proportion to their commitment to excellence regardless of their chosen field of endeavor." It does not matter what your background is or your chosen field of endeavor; you can improve your personal and business life by applying these time-honored principles of thinking of yourself as an entrepreneur and the president of your own corporation.

It's time to reevaluate some of the decisions you've made about your talents and goals. Consider whether you are really on the right track to create the future you want. Your responsibility is to choose resources to support you, create a purpose that gives your life direction, and love yourself enough to be committed to go for what makes you happy. One of your strongest assets in dealing with the future is realizing that you have the power to write your own life's script and change it when necessary. Seeing yourself as an entrepreneur, a person who moves with the times, gives you the leverage to control your destiny.

_10_
CREATING PROSPERITY
REGARDLESS OF THE ECONOMY

My sincere desire is to share with you strategies to empower you and help you to gain the confidence that comes from understanding how manifesting works; to use the tools offered here to create whatever you want; to take your vision, your dreams, your hopes, and your fantasies and make them real; to take responsibility for your life and enjoy the aliveness and the personal and professional growth you can have; to achieve new levels of clarity with exactly what you want and to be in control of your own life.

As you read this chapter, open your mind to the perspective that creating wealth and abundance has a lot to do with internal decisions and external knowledge and little to do with the state of the national economy. We must rise above the popular belief that it is necessary to be affected by the economy. Abundance is a mind-set, not an external condition that controls your destiny. This information can help you claim the abundance you so richly deserve. There are no limits to what we can create because we have unlimited resources around us.

Let's begin by defining wealth. Wealth is not just money, because creating money alone will not always bring you happiness. Wealth is being at peace with yourself and feeling fulfilled in what you do. It is enjoying and appreciating your life, your family, and your career.

Catherine Ponder, a woman who is very admired, has written a number of successful books on prosperity. In one of them she says, "Prosperity is more than money, wealth, and financial security, it is the way you live your life and the way you focus your life energy, it is the balance of what you can and cannot control, it is loving yourself and others, it is counting your blessings and enjoying who and what you currently are now." One of the main reasons for this particular chapter is to share with you the need for something called "prosperity consciousness" in your life. Increasing this level of awareness enables you to create more self-confidence, self-trust, and self-esteem. These new empowering traits will help you generate and create wealth and financial security.

The definition of the word "prosper" is to flourish, succeed, and thrive, to experience favorable results to get what you want out of life. It is more than wealth and financial security. Ralph Waldo Emerson described prosperity as the law of compensation whereby like attracts like, and what you radiate out in your thoughts, feelings, mental pictures, and words you also attract into your life. The truth is that we are where we are in our life at this moment because of our past programming.

Our educational system does not offer courses on creating prosperity or abundance, so we are basically left to guess at the best ways to create wealth. Unless you have deliberately sought out books, tapes, or seminars or have been fortunate enough to have had mentors in your life who have shared with you this valuable information, you were on your own. You may have thought that just being lucky or working hard or investing wisely would create wealth. You will agree that all these things are clearly helpful; however, I would like to share with you the knowledge I have learned from being a sincere student of prosperity. I have read every book possible on prosperity, listened to every expert attentively, gone to countless seminars, and experimented with many different techniques. The following ideas from my personal experience have worked for me and, if you are willing to try them, will also work for you.

To benefit from this information, you must have an open mind to consider new concepts. Actually these concepts are not really new; it is just that we were not taught them in school or exposed to them by some other influential environment. We have to start by letting go of old beliefs that no longer serve us. You see, the more open-minded you are, the more opportunities, thoughts, feelings, and perceptions can come to you.

History has recorded that more millionaires were created during the Great Depression than at any other time because of the infamous "poor economy." The people who believed in themselves were willing to take calculated risks. They took advantage of low prices, cheap labor, and available government funding for chosen projects. These people made tremendous amounts of money because they believed in themselves, looked for opportunities, and *had prosperity consciousness*. They did not let fate control their futures—they took charge of their own destinies with their thoughts and their actions!

Today there are many successful people who say they make more money during a time of recession than when the economy is booming. They say it is because people run scared and sell out easily for less. The mass population tends to buy into what the media reports and financial experts' predictions of how bad the economy is or will be. When you buy into mass beliefs of poverty, you unknowingly limit the opportunities you could see for creating money or happiness.

We are all victims of old programming. From previous chapters you will recall how our self-image is created between the ages three to seven by our teachers, parents, peers, and society. Some of the limiting programming we received on a daily basis were statements like *"the rich only get richer"* and *"this is a tough world"* and *"money is the root of all evil."* You may not even be conscious of it when you hear yourself talking and saying things like *"everything happens to me," "the other guy is always lucky and gets all the breaks,"* or *"I can't win for losing."*

For prosperity consciousness to work, start to pay attention to the quality of information you put into your computer, your brain; it truly is your success mechanism. Pay even closer attention to your self-talk because it is your self-talk that programs you for either poverty consciousness or prosperity consciousness.

You Are the Source of Your Wealth

To have abundance in any area of your life, you must take 100-percent responsibility for your own abundance because *you are the source of your own riches.* You will not find the source in your job or your investments or even your loved ones. The truth is that your job can be eliminated, you could lose your investments, and your loved ones could lose their means of supporting you. There is no security in life except for the abilities, talents, and skills you have to take care of yourself and the attitude that you will do whatever it takes. The greatest power we have to direct and control our life is through our thoughts. *Thoughts are real.* They are like sunshine and radiate out. Each one of us acts as a powerful broadcasting station sending out positive or negative vibrations. The universal law, not a concept, is that like attracts like and our thoughts attract people and things that match those thoughts.

Everything we know in today's world was once an idea or thought before it could exist in reality. Cars, electricity, planes, computers, even the style of clothing we wear or furniture in your home or office had to be created in someone's mind. One of the greatest rules of success for creating abundance is to focus on what you want instead of what you don't want. Whatever you focus on is what you will get—*energy follows thought.* The more you focus on being poor, the poorer you will become. The more you focus on abundance and the more you picture it, the more you will do to get it. But you must take responsibility for your dreams and your goals and be willing to take action to attain them.

Release Limiting Programs

Dwelling on your problems only creates more. It also leaves you tired and feeling hopeless. And when you are preoccupied with negative thoughts, you are not doing things that will allow you to create abundance or success or wealth in your life. Here is a startling quote by the author of *Unlimited Power*, Anthony Robbins: "It is not a lack of ideas on earth, but a lack of energy to create them."

Pay attention to the caliber of information you put into your mind by choosing and controlling your thoughts. The chapter entitled "Your Declaration of Independence" describes the technique of using pattern interrupts on yourself. You must also replace those thoughts that do not serve you. When you say things like *"I don't have enough money,"* start to replace that with *"I have an abundance of money."* Our positive thoughts are more powerful than our negative ones, so remember that you can reprogram your computer with your thoughts. Use the supporting statements mentioned earlier called Declarations. They can serve and help you create your own destiny since you are the controller of your wealth through your thoughts. Obviously your intention is to create abundance and prosperity, to obtain the things you want in your life. By using Declarations you will actually be reprogramming your subconscious mind to accept these new thoughts as reality. As you imprint this information on your mind, it begins to create changes in your life to match this new inner reality.

Your goal is to *focus on the new.* Take on the spirit of *creating something new* rather than changing or resisting what is now. Always act to give yourself permission and make believe it is true right now. Create the feeling you want to experience so your subconscious knows what to imprint. Here are some examples of Declarations that you can use to make you feel more prosperous:

I have the prosperity habit.
I am in this world to experience and enjoy success.
I have every natural right to be wealthy
    and successful.
I am confident of my talents to create success.
I have great enthusiasm and confidence.
I choose to be prosperous.
I love myself more and more daily.
I have the energy, resources and time
    to be successful and prosperous.
I am more intelligent every day in every way thinking of new creative ways to attract money.

*I am projecting an image of power and confidence
that attracts to me the right people and the right
situations.*
I am willing to be powerful and successful.
I know I have valuable contributions.
I reinforce my successes as I correct my errors.

Whatever we think about ourselves and our abilities
will determine how successful and prosperous we become.

Your Imagination—The Workshop of Your Mind

Another strategy for creating abundance in your life, in
all areas, is to use your imagination, the workshop of your
mind. It is not bound by limiting beliefs, fears, or past
conditioning. Remember those dreams you had at another
time in your life but have forgotten to have enthusiasm
for? Now, dream and think even bigger than before. Since
we are self-fulfilling prophecies, move past old pictures in
your mind and boundaries you have set up limiting what
you can achieve, have, create, and deserve. Those limiting
beliefs were yesterday's thoughts. You now have the resources to create and tap into that unused 85 percent of potential
(talent, ability, and creativity). Visualization gives you the
ability to unleash your greatest power, your potential.

In Catherine Ponder's book, *The Dynamic Laws of
Prosperity,* she says, "Authorities who study the mind
believe that man can create anything he can imagine—the
mental image does make the emotions and experiences of
man's life and affairs, that man's only limitation lies in
the negative use of his imagination." In other words, if
there is failure and lack in your life, it is because you
first imagined it in your mind. The imagination is a much
stronger force than willpower—and when the imagination
and will are in conflict, imagination always wins out.

She went on to suggest that you, instead of battling with
poverty, failure, and financial lack, which often only mul-
tiplies your problems, begin to use the indirect method—that
of quietly, deliberately and persistently imagining your goal.
Success is created mentally first.

You will then create what you want faster if your intent to have it is very clear and strong. So when opportunities arise, you are alert and can take advantage of them. You will be willing to take calculated risks. If you are not absolutely sure of your desires, opportunities will pass you by, obstacles will stand in your way, and you will tend to give up quickly. Right now you are the sum total of all of your past choices. What you have and where you are in life are the results of the decisions you have made in using or choosing not to use your talents.

Charles Fillmore once described the terrific power of the imagination when he wrote, "Imagination gives man the ability to project and rise above all limitations." Your power of imagination, when given definite pictures to imprint, will instruct the subconscious mind to get busy producing definitive results for you.

One very important thing—*don't compromise in your mental pictures.* Imagine what you really want—not just what you think you can have. If you fill your imagination with half-hearted mental pictures, that's the kind of results you'll get.

Personal Development

Today we no longer have to be passive about our choices. We can be proactive. We want to consciously examine how we can better use our life energy mentally, physically, and emotionally to create value to our lives and others. There is a wonderful book called *Creating Money,* by Sanaya Roman and Duane Packer. It says, "Rather than determine success in terms of the concrete things it might represent to you, such as how much money you have in the bank or what kind of house or car you have, be willing to expand your definition of success to also include personal development." Personal development is found in transforming an old habit or a negative belief, releasing fear, doing things you love, developing and recognizing your special talents, making a contribution to others, loving and respecting yourself and others, and growing and learning from all of your experiences.

Enjoy Your Successes

If we really face life and look back on what we have been able to accomplish in the past, we are already successful. You already have people who love you, the freedom to make choices that serve you, knowledge, and experience. It's time for you to recognize your own unlimited opportunities. Start to catch yourself doing things right and congratulate yourself often. Begin to appreciate yourself and count your blessings. Isn't it interesting how most people look ahead to the next mountain peak in life, without ever taking the time to appreciate the heights they just conquered?

By appreciating and acknowledging your successes, you will not only enjoy them more, but you will create more energy and confidence for yourself to create even more success, abundance, and prosperity for your future. Also, it is time for us to look at the small things that give us so much pleasure, joy, and happiness—such as a sunset, a great meal, playing with your children, making love, or reading a good book. That is the wealth of life.

By dwelling on feelings of success, you imprint on your computer much more confidence to handle the challenges of the future. All of your energy will create some type of result. If you start to focus and remember the feelings of mastery in different areas of your life, you will cause an imprint on your computer and help you create greater success for the future. Your thoughts *do* create your beliefs, and *your beliefs create your reality.*

Your beliefs about money will determine how you relate to it and how you spend it. If you see the world as having unlimited resources, which it does, then you tend to feel more relaxed about money. You know you can earn it or attract it whenever you need it, if you're willing to work wisely. However, if you think you can receive money only by working extremely hard through toil and sweat, then that is exactly what you'll end up doing. Why not make life a little easier for ourselves? Why exhaust ourselves with so much toil and sweat when we could apply our mental capacities and achieve even more? It has been taught to us over the ages by the great teachers that we can learn to create our destiny through our thoughts and use our thought energy rather than physical effort to produce results that go beyond anything you will be able to create with just physical effort alone.

Plant Seeds for Success

Another concept about abundance is planting seeds. I learned one of nature's most important lessons while growing up on a farm on Chuckatuck Creek. My father was a farmer, and the lessons and experiences I learned while living on the farm were in understanding that there were seasons when he planted and seasons when he harvested. In between he made sure he weeded, watered, and nurtured the seeds he'd planted. He knew that not all of them would come up or survive the weather, and he always made sure to plant more than he needed because he knew the rules of nature. We were also acutely aware that if you didn't plant seeds, there would be no harvest!

Even now those lessons have served me very well in my life. I am always amazed how people live their daily life but do not plant seeds for their future. I'm not sure what they think will happen, or who they expect to take care of them. Maybe they're thinking their parents or the government will save them. Occasionally they may try a single new idea, but if that doesn't pan out, they give up. One of the most crucial strategies that all entrepreneurial and successful people use is that they *keep planting many seeds and trying new things until they find the right one.*

They plant seeds in all different kinds of ways. They cultivate contacts with other people, asking for references, support, and ideas. They plant seeds by learning as much as they can about areas they're interested in. Successful people plant seeds of encouragement for themselves by building support systems or belonging to organizations and clubs that allow them to grow and meet people with similar interests. They plant seeds of success by being honest, having integrity, doing more than expected, and doing first-class jobs because they know their reputations are everything and that word-of-mouth advertising is very power-ful. Smart people plant seeds of success by looking and acting the part. It is a proven fact that the better you dress, the more successful you will feel and the more confident you will appear. Since we get to create our reality by what we do, it is crucial that the seeds we plant reinforce where we want to go. You cannot get something for nothing—you must sow before you reap.

The theme of "you must invest before receiving" is an ancient one. You *will* reap what you sow. Please keep in mind that, regardless of the environment, you must continue planting seeds. There will always be a natural rhythm to life. Every business has ebb and flow. People have different cycles in life. Our challenge is to be aware of the natural cycles and to not become discouraged when those cycles are down. All things on earth are cyclical and all phases of life are simply temporary. When there is a short-term shortage, that is the time to plant more seeds and do the things you've put off. Spend more time investing in your mind, learning and exploring new concepts. That might also be the time to take a needed vacation to renew yourself for the next phase.

Whatever you do, keep your attitude positive so that you can turn things around when given the opportunity because worrying is nonproductive. Focus all that energy that you've used worrying in the past and apply it in ways that will allow you to gain experience to serve you. Here is a great old saying: "Worry is like a rocking chair; it gives you something to do but gets you nowhere!" When you worry, you actually block your thinking from creativity and productivity. Don't forget to be aware of your words. Don't speak of lack or dwell on your failures and financial problems. Words are very powerful to the subconscious mind. Instead, talk about what is going on in your life right now that is great. When you meet people and they ask how things are, tell them things are terrific! Talk about what you are excited about and your dreams and visions, talk about how positive and excited you are about your future. Expressing your enthusiasm aloud adds momentum to your progress.

Do What You Love

One of the most important strategies that appears in every book on prosperity is *do what you love and the money will come.* Confucius said, "Choose a job you love and you will never work a day in your life." By working and doing something you really love and enjoy spending your time and energy doing, you start to feel more alive as if you've tapped into your purpose on earth. You radiate more happiness and joy than you ever believed possible. There is a sense of fulfillment about working at what you love most.

You also become more at peace with yourself. When you start to use your natural-born talents and skills in your life's work, it doesn't mean you are bound to one job or one career forever. You can be if you want to, depending on what makes you happy, but be aware of the fact that every position you've ever had, every job you've ever worked, and everything you've ever done teaches you information that will help you advance to the next step. The bottom line is, to be able to spend your life in your own way is true success.

The way I have chosen to spend my life is to be a communicator. I have done this in many different ways and will continue to do it in many different ways. First, I began my career in sales serving people by supplying information and services that create value for them. Then, as a professional photographer, I traveled around the world shooting landscape photography, thus communicating through images and pictures. I have also written articles and books to communicate information to share about how to be more successful and fulfilled in life. Today I am producing and hosting television shows, where I can communicate many different topics. And of course, I also personally speak to groups all over the world. I develop and produce audio learning cassettes and videos. I have found many different avenues to be a communicator and express my purpose.

I can honestly say that every avenue I have used so far, and the avenues I will use in the future, will help me evolve into an even more successful person. I really don't believe I would be where I am today if I had not done such a variety of jobs in the past. As you can see, those avenues have given me a well of experience that I draw from and use every day. We are all very special and unique. We all have our own special contribution to make to mankind.

Follow Your Heart

Many times in our careers and lives, we feel unfulfilled and unhappy because we have set goals that don't answer our deepest needs, whether we selected those goals for ourselves or allowed others to do it for us by their influence on our choices. For example, my brother Gray went to school with a very talented young man, John, whose father and grandfather were very successful attorneys. As a small child, even before he began school, John was conditioned that he was expected to become part of the family law firm. Although throughout his schooling he had shown an unbelievable talent for art, he was never encouraged by his family to use these talents.

After John graduated law school and joined the family's law practice, he became increasingly unhappy and unfulfilled with his work and life. As he continued, he became overweight and developed high blood pressure and ulcers. Eventually, after ten years of frustration, John had a nervous breakdown. Upon recovering, he left his family's business and began his own art school for children. Today he is not making the same money as he would have as a lawyer, but he is a totally changed man. For the first time in his life, he is happy, healthy, full of life, and at peace with himself. He is now building a new life that suits his inner desires and talents. He has found a career that gives him peace of mind and joy. That clearly ranks as one of the most important measures of success for anyone in life.

We cannot go through life fulfilling other people's desires and expect to be happy ourselves. A winner is someone who sets goals, commits to those goals, and then pursues those goals with all the ability given him. To be in complete harmony with ourselves is much more important than impressing others. Peace of mind simply means that we are free from anger, guilt, and fear. To achieve such a state of mind allows us to use the unlimited potential we all have within us. You have to start to live from your own heart and *do what you love.*

Attitude Adjustment Time

There is a quote from Herbert Swope that really makes sense. He said, "I cannot give you a formula for success, but I can give you the formula for failure; try to please everybody." Suppose at this time you have to stay where you are at work because you are only a couple of years way from retirement, or you are supporting a young family, or you don't know what else to do at this time? Did you realize opinion polls have found that over one half of the people in North America dislike huge parts of their jobs?

Nancy Anderson, author of *Work With Passion*, says "In the 90's, people are demanding satisfaction and meaning from their work." And it's a well-established fact that you'll be much more productive if you love what you're doing. Abraham Lincoln said, "Most people are about as happy as they make up their minds to be." A researcher of work attitudes, Howard Schecter, said, "What's ultimately separating us from our work are our own attitudes." It's the commonly held notion that work is a drag or the boss is a problem. Let go of those ideas, and you may discover the work itself isn't the problem—the real way to make changes in the workplace is to start by first looking inside at how we think about our jobs. It's in your attitude. Success in life is *80 percent attitude* and *20 percent aptitude.*

In the book *Do What You Love, The Money Will Follow,* Marsha Sinetar says, "Most of us resist our jobs and that benefits no one." Everyone has chores and responsibilities we don't like. The antidote is to choose to do whatever you are doing now—after all, if it's worth doing, do it well. If you're cleaning house, really clean it, getting into those nooks and crannies; if you're exercising, go the extra mile and realize the benefit of a healthy workout. If you can choose to do your work responsibly and consciously, and that means willingly putting your full focus into the task you are engaged in, then you can do this even while looking for something better!

Dr. Christopher Hegarty, consultant and author of *How to Manage Your Boss*, said "A widely held thought is that some jobs are beyond loving or even liking but that's erroneous. It's your choice how you view your work." Many people have bought into the idea that you do as little as you can for as much money as you can get and still get home as early as possible. *Nobody wins that way.* Those who try to experience the joy of their labor, *find it*—even in supposedly "meaningless jobs" (by other people's standards).

There are some very positive effects to changing your attitudes about work. You'll have more energy—you'll take more risks—you'll feel more positive and live in the moment—you'll find a sense of participation and ownership. Your productivity will increase and your prosperity will increase because you have created value to yourself and others! There are a number of powerful strategies that can aid you in creating a life that is filled with happiness, health, and wealth. You do not have to have millions in the bank to live a wealthy life. Life is in the perception. You can consciously and deliberately direct your thoughts and actions toward living the good life by using these powerful strategies.

STRATEGY ONE
Law of Vacuum

One of the first strategies to create prosperity is to get rid of what you don't want in your life to make room for what you do want. It is said that nature abhors a vacuum. To have the opportunity to attract what you do want, such as a better relationship, more attractive clothes or furniture, you must make room for your desires to manifest.

No matter what your economic status, there are probably many possessions that you're not using, which are just cluttering up your life and space. If you want new clothes yet every time you go into your closet you have to pry an outfit out because there are so many clothes jammed into it, you will have no motivation to go out and invest in clothes that make you feel attractive and confident. You must also keep in mind that you only have so much life energy. If you're using that energy looking at garments you really don't like, have gone out of style, or that no longer fit, you experience frustration, guilt, and/or other negative feelings. They rob you of time and energy.

Another example is drawers full of junk. Every time you go to find something, you first have to wade through a lot of useless junk wasting your time. The same goes for files in your desk—it's hard to be organized and feel in control of your paper work if your files are loaded with dated, useless information.

If you're living in fear of lack and tightly holding on to everything—your material possessions, your time, your love, your energy or ideas, you're shutting yourself off from the flow of life. When you dam up a stream, the water becomes stagnant. When you close off your life, *you* become stagnant. The more unwanted things clutter your life, the less room there will be for the things you want to be able to appear.

A great universal secret of prosperity is passing along to others those things you no longer need. The more you give away of those excess material possessions, the more love, appreciation, and praise the world will surprise you with by increasing your abundance in all areas of your life.

Homework Assignment

Pick a different area in your home or office and give yourself permission to go through your material possessions making two piles: one to throw away, the other to either give away or sell; with what you decide to keep you will organize in a manner that makes you feel in control.

If there are clothes in your closet that you have not worn in the last twenty-four months—get rid of them! If there are clothes you don't like and which don't give you a good feeling when you wear them—get rid of them. If there are clothes needing repair, have them repaired. Your one exception—you can keep your wedding dress or tuxedo!

Don't forget to clean out your attic and garage; inevitably there are things you're keeping that would cost more to repair than replace—throw them out or give them away.

Get rid of old furniture, toys, office files, magazines, and newspapers. Clear out the junk that robs you of your energy and time whenever you see or think about it. Unclutter your life with the tangibles and intangibles that are no longer adding to your well-being. New substances, new relationships, and new opportunities do not flow easily into a cluttered environment.

Another important homework assignment is to allow yourself to gently move away from acquaintances and friends who are no longer really friends. Just because you were close and had a lot in common at one time does not mean that you're destined to be friends forever. Give yourself permission to recognize and let go of relationships that have grown in different directions. By continuing to spend your time with people with whom you no longer have rewarding relationships, you are preventing yourself from having opportunities to meet and spend time with people that you really would enjoy or from whom you would learn.

When you move things, people, or situations that no longer serve you out of your life, you're clearing the way for what you *do* want. It's difficult to know what you do want until you get rid of what you don't want or what is no longer working.

STRATEGY TWO
Power of Forgiveness

Another important rule of creating a happier, healthier, and more successful life is to be aware of the how you are using your life energy; you are made up of mental, physical, emotional, and spiritual life energy. If you're using your energy holding on to past grudges, anger, guilty feelings, or negative feelings, you're wasting your life energy. Using your life energy to hold on to negative thoughts prevents you from creating new ideas and then having the energy to take action on them. The antidote is to forgive yourself and forgive other people. Many people have a hard time with the concept of forgiveness. But the point is that you do not have to condone what wrongs you perceive others to have done. You're not forgiving them for their sake. You are giving yourself a gift by forgiving them for yourself. Forgiveness is releasing the thoughts, grudges, and anger that takes up your time and energy. Through forgiveness and release of negative energy, your power of attracting good is greatly increased.

STRATEGY THREE
The Power of Appreciation

Not only do we want to stop talking and thinking economic lack and limitation because of the effects on our subconscious, we also want to start to live as richly as possible on what we already have.

It always amazes me how people go through life saving their best clothes, china, silver, and/or good furniture and then die without ever really enjoying the pleasures right there within their reach. If *you* are one of those people who use "the good stuff" only on holidays or special occasions, you most likely enjoy them only a few times each year. If you think about it, that means that, in a one-year period, you may have allowed yourself to enjoy the finer things in your life for just a few days! In the overall album of life, there is something wrong with that picture! *Life is for living*—it should be celebrated and enjoyed!

May I suggest that, instead of following other people's traditions, you start today to create more feelings of prosperity in your life by giving yourself permission to use your "good stuff" more often. Treat yourself and your family—have dinner with your best silver and china and eat by candlelight once a week if possible. This gives your subconscious the message that you are blessed, you *do* deserve the best in life. Isn't it interesting how so many people save their material possessions so their relatives can quarrel over them after they pass away? I am suggesting that you actually live and enjoy what material possessions you now have.

The same thought goes for your clothes. Why is it we walk around our home before our most cherished loved ones in the worst clothes we own? Why do we save our good clothes to impress strangers? Who's more important anyway (food for thought for you)? Consider wearing some of those clothes in your closet before they go out of style! That's why you own them—to enjoy them. Again let me emphasize that the way you feel about yourself has a huge impact on your state of mind. If you feel you look good, you have more confidence. When you have more confidence, you'll naturally take more calculated risks in life. You'll be more optimistic and in turn see more ideas and ways to capitalize on those ideas. Which of course gives you the opportunity to make more money, meet better contacts, and create new ventures. This is what creating prosperity in your life is all about.

It's amazing how most people overlook the small things you can do for your well-being that really make a difference in how you will perceive the world. When you carry within you thoughts of potential happiness, health, and wealth, they radiate outward into your world and will attract like results into your life. You have to *feel* successful, worthy, and blessed to be able to attract it into your life.

STRATEGY FOUR
Prosperity Is A Planned Result

Prosperity is the result of deliberate thought and action. As the Bible promises, ask and it shall be given you, seek and ye shall find, knock and the door shall be opened. If your desires are not definitive, it's very hard for your subconscious to give you innovative ideas, directions, or answers to create the life style you want for yourself. If you interview or read about the most prominent and successful people, you will find the majority use a technique for creating their desires—they *write down what they want*.

There is magic in putting ideas on paper.

Begin making a list of all the things you wish cleared up and eradicated from your life. This list should include everything from old relationships, old habits, and fears to material objects. This exercise will empower you to have a clearer picture of what you do want.

I recommend that you start a new daily ritual of sitting down first thing in the morning and listing your goals for that day. It is a very effective way of invoking the creative law of prosperity. By focusing your attention at the beginning of every day on what to do with your life energy, you give your computer, your brain, direction and it always follows the most powerful directions given to it. By simply taking a couple of minutes first thing in the morning to make a list of your desired accomplishments, you'll be in control of your day. By spending your life energy wisely you are giving yourself a wonderful gift—a new lease on life. Before you know it, this new strategy will put you in control of your life.

STRATEGY FIVE
The Prosperity Law of Goodwill and Love

No matter what you know about prosperity laws, if you're not able to work and live harmoniously with other people, you won't truly have abundance in your life. Your wealth will feel empty. I have heard it said that approximately 15 percent of your financial success is due to your technical abilities and 85 percent to your ability to get along and work well with people. Charles Fillmore's comment on the power of love was, "You may trust love to get you out of your difficulties. There is nothing too hard for it to accomplish for you if you put your confidence in it."

The world is a looking glass, and it gives back to you a reflection of your attitude. So the bottom line is: if you want a friend, you must first be a friend; if you want people to be happy about your successes, you must also be happy for the success of others. When speaking of other people, speak only in terms of their successes or positive traits. Don't gossip or waste time reinforcing negative information—free yourself from petty thinking. If you know someone who failed in some way but is clearly trying to make a comeback, support them by ignoring their past and emphasize their present good!

One of the most upsetting traits I notice in many people is their disdain and bitterness if others achieve something or acquire material possessions that they themselves have not achieved or acquired. Many of these people try to find ways to put those individuals down, to belittle them or find fault. It's as if they believe that the world is limited and so, if these other people profit, then there are no benefits left for them.

Many people spend their energies on bickering, jealousies and petty criticisms. I cannot emphasize enough how the power of your thinking is an instrument for success or failure. You are now the sum total of your past thoughts. The thoughts you have from this day forward will determine your future and the amount of happiness and prosperity you experience. I want to impress on you that if you truly desire to have prosperity in your life you must start to be happy for others' successes. Life is like a boomerang—what you toss out into the world comes back into your own life. You've heard the phrase "what goes around comes around"? When you have thoughts of jealously and revenge you are actually attracting that energy to yourself. In reality, the world is an unlimiting place where you can create whatever it is you truly want.

Free yourself from criticism of yourself and others. Be different from those who are prone to finding fault with everything, unless you want to remain with them. Dare to act and think in a new manner. Deliberately employ prosperous thinking as your ally for success, therefore freeing yourself from limitations, lack, and failure. The famous philosopher James Allen said, "Through his thoughts, man holds the key to every situation and contains within himself that transforming and regenerative agency by which he may make himself what he wills."

STRATEGY SIX
The Law of Self-Love

One of the most important rules of success and prosperity is that you must learn to love and appreciate yourself. You *are worthy* of all the world's riches. To be able to have anything in life, you must first believe that you are worthy of it. If you do not believe you are worthy of living the good life, you will unconsciously sabotage yourself and your efforts. It is a well-known fact that human beings strive to prove ourselves right. As Richard Bach said, "Argue for your limitations and they will be yours."

Many people have decided as a life's theme that they don't deserve what they really want in life. Maybe that was the message that your parents gave you or maybe you just picked up that belief from your environment, but I have to ask you these very life-changing questions right now: How is this belief serving you or your family? What will this belief cost you in time and lost opportunities for fun and enjoyment? Is this belief really worth hanging on to?

The answer for me was "No." I made a conscious decision that life was too short to feel unworthy of enjoying the blessings and fruits of the world. Hopefully this chapter will create the desire for you to truly love and nurture yourself to allow true prosperity to enhance your life.

Do things daily that improve your self-esteem. One of the most important ways to improve your life is to expose yourself to information every day that will remind you of how worthy you are of having whatever you are willing to create for yourself. The power of your mind is the instrument of your success or failure, and happiness or unhappiness in life.

Don't associate with others who dwell on the negative; stay away from negative newspaper, magazine, television, and radio information that drags you down and makes you focus on what is not working in life. Get out of old ruts of thinking, acting, and behaving. For the next 21 days create a new routine for yourself, do things differently. A rut is a living death. By simply changing your habits, you give yourself the opportunity to enjoy new things. You allow yourself to see new opportunities and you recreate the spark in your life that makes life fun again. It's really sad that most people go through life unconsciously. They get up at the same time every morning, eat the same breakfast, drive the same route to work, eat lunch with the same people, talk about the same worn, tired subjects, and then go home and follow the same routine night after night. These are the same people who say life is no longer fun. They complain there is nothing to do, and that life is boring. Their relationships are dying on the vine from lack of stimulation.

Today *is* the first day of the rest of your life, so do something different! Try changing your routine—experiment by wearing different outfits, trying new foods, going out to eat in a new place, shopping in a different part of town. Invite over a neighbor whom you've not really gotten to know before. Go to a museum or to the library and read books on subjects that you've never read before, even try a new hair cut. Just do something different every day for next 21 days and see and feel how much more alive you will become!!

STRATEGY SEVEN
Take Action

A formerly well-to-do man had fallen on hard times. He became bitter about his current situation and turned to God to save him. Night after night he began praying to win the lottery. The next time the lottery was drawn, he did not win. Again he got on his knees and said, "God, I haven't got a job and I need to win." Again, the lottery was drawn and he did not win. The man was by now becoming frustrated and angry. He said to God, "I must win the lottery; my rent is due, I don't have enough money to eat this week. Give me a break, let me win the lottery!" And out of the dark a strong voice said, *"You give me a break, if you want to win the lottery you at least have to buy a ticket!"*

This is a silly story but it has much truth to it. Many people think they will be saved by some outside source and never take action to look for that source or work toward their goals. The reality of life is that we have to be 100 percent responsible for the results we get in our life. If we want to create more wealth, we have to figure out ways to be more productive and creative and then *take action* on those ideas! The average person is always waiting for something to happen instead of working to make things happen. For every person who dreams of making a fortune, there are thousands of people dreaming of winning the lottery.

George Bernard Shaw said, "The people who get on in this world are the people who get up and look for the circumstances they want and if they cannot find them—make them." A long time ago I decided that I wanted to live my life doing things I like. I wanted to control my time and my energy. To have the ability to control my time and energy, I had to pay the price of being self-employed.

But whether you are self-employed or work for someone else at this time in your life, you must start to take action to create whatever you want out of life. My deepest desire for this book is to be able to share tools, resources, and experiences to empower you to have the courage and motivation to do just that—simply take action.

I want to assure you, I do not suggest that you try to take huge steps. You can build your confidence and your beliefs in yourself by simply taking small steps in the direction of your goal(s). It's very interesting to note that changing just a few small actions or habits in your life will compound and in a few months those changes can have dramatic effects.

As an example, one of the many strategies that enabled me to create more prosperity in my life was simple but had a tremendous impact on my future. Many books on prosperity state that it is important to not program any type of negative information in the mind first thing in the morning. One of my habits for many years had been to get up in the early morning, and spend thirty minutes each day having my coffee and reading the entire newspaper. Little did I realize that I was loading my computer with hundreds of reasons to be afraid of the world. Without being aware of the consequences of my actions, I now realize how my fears kept me from taking action on many of my ideas. Since hindsight is always 20/20, I realize that my reading negative news dampened much of my positive attitude and stifled much of my creativity for the day.

No one's kidding you that habits aren't hard to break, but I made a decision to stop reading the newspaper and listening to the news first thing in the morning. I still wanted to sit down and enjoy my coffee while reading something so I simply substituted self-help or inspirational books instead of the newspaper.

I can honestly say that modifying that particular action has reaped huge rewards for me in my enthusiasm for life and has improved my appreciation of the blessings around me. I believe with all my heart that I became more productive and creative in my energies because I didn't have fears and doubts reinforced by outside sources before I began my work day.

Over the years I have known and observed many people who are always telling me about their research and plans to go into a selected field or start a chosen business. These people are continually gathering more and more information. They waste time and energy talking about what they are going to do one day: *"When I get enough money I'll open that shop, When my kids are old enough, When the economy gets better, When I have time, When I retire. . ."*

What is interesting about listening to most of these people is that I know they'll never do it. They've gathered all the information they need—now all they need is to *do something! Take action!* I'll concede that, many times when you first want to make changes in your life and take action, the steps you take may not always be the perfect choices. But at least the activity gets your momentum going and you have begun. My strongest advice for creating prosperity in your life is to take some positive actions today that will, over time, create some new results for you.

CHAPTER
-11-
REDEFINING WEALTH: DETERMINE WHAT SUCCESS MEANS TO YOU

In the chapter entitled "Creating Prosperity Regardless of the Economy," you received the internal keys to creating prosperity. You do have the power to live a life filled with abundance. In this chapter, we will talk about the choices you make with your resources: your time, energy and money.

Faith Popcorn's book *The Popcorn Report* says, "We are asking ourselves what is real, what is honest, what is quality, what is valued, what is really important. We are trading in the rewards of traditional success in favor of slower pace and quality of life." She went on to say, "In the seventies, we worked to live. In the eighties, we lived to work. Now we simply want to live—long and well. We are asking ourselves, is all this stress really worth the reward? Isn't this life I'm living shortening my life? Is this all there is?"

One of our options to deal with the changing world is to develop a new strategy for living more simply—allowing ourselves to feel more in control. You do not have to listen to the news or read the newspapers to understand that we can no longer depend on our employer or the government to take care of us. In this decade, we will see a turnaround from fast-track living to a resurrection of values. We must begin to see ourselves as pioneers carving out a new way to live life in the midst of global uncertainty.

Madison Avenue will not like what I am about to suggest because their goal is to entice us to buy, buy, buy—but I propose a new way of looking at wealth. What if, for instance, instead of continuously striving for bigger homes, more elaborate furnishings, and more grandiose life style, you were to pause for a moment and ask yourself what wealth means to you?

People identify money with all sorts of wonderful things, pleasure, prestige, quality, power, and security. Many of us get locked into a lifelong struggle to obtain the freedom that money is supposed to bring. For example, although we might have the material possessions that are typically associated with wealth—nice house, a luxury car, lots of good clothes, and perhaps a boat or vacation home—we sometimes painfully find out that the "more is better" mentality leads to misery. That's because no matter what we get, it's never enough. If you've just taken ownership of a new car, there's yet a bigger, better car to yearn for. Happiness seems to be in the next object we want.

How often have you struggled through your workday wishing you could spend less time working for money and more time enjoying life? Too often, as we are finding out today, the stress of a fast-paced life style, the long hours spent working overtime—all the entanglements of living beyond your means—has a big price. The price is your peace of mind and *all* of your time. When your primary focus in life is to buy, buy, buy, it's easy to overlook the simpler pleasures: those of quiet time alone or with your loved ones away from the hustle and bustle, the joy of gardening, or watching your children play.

You see, Madison Avenue would have us believe that if we make a lot of money all our problems will be solved. But money, in and of itself, never brings true wealth. The old adage "money isn't everything" is very true. Many people who by all outward standards are incredibly successful and prosperous are inwardly miserable. In reality, wealth has little to do with money. It is a state of mind. Wealth is being at peace with yourself and feeling fulfilled in whatever you do. In fact, you may be able to create a great deal more wealth in your life if, instead of focusing on accumulating more money and material goods—and thus, more debt—you start to live more simply and more easily within your means. You have then merely transformed your relationship with money.

I agree with many experts on living well who stress that financial independence has nothing to do with being rich. It is simply knowing when you have enough. I'm not suggesting that everyone arrive at the same definition of what is enough; however, I am suggesting that you become clear about what is real for you and within your financial means. Just a short decade ago, we consumers were over-extending ourselves to buy showy luxuries; today we are over-extended-out! We were looking for an emotional fix and indulgence of ego expression. Today we have to balance the cost benefit for our gratification. Is the stress of debt worth it?

As we apply this new definition to our individual prosperity, we must recognize that a huge part of being wealthy is being free enough of debt and worry so we are able to enjoy the life we already have. There is an ancient scripture that reads, "A wealthy man is a man who is content with what he has." To put that in today's terms, I would say, "A wealthy person is a person free enough of the stress of debt to have the time and attitude necessary to enjoy the richness of the present life." The world often defines wealth purely in terms of money, influence, and material possessions. Here's a suggestion for you—temporarily disregard the opinions of the world and consider new options to feel rich.

It is only within yourself that you are able to find empowerment. To do so, you must learn to take your power back from the world and return it to its proper place—that is, within the ultimate "powerhouse" of the individual self. Any time our happiness or sense of self is being defined by someone or something outside of ourselves, we are giving away our power. Since happiness and true success come from our own sense of empowerment in the world, when we give away our power we lose our happiness.

A New Perspective

According to Vicki Robin and Joe Dominquez, authors of the successful book *Your Money Or Your Life*, "Grabbing all you can is out; making do with what you have is in. Instant gratification is out; long term gains are in. Conspicuous is out: consciousness is in." They insist this is not a fad. "It's a philosophy upon which this country was founded. It's about squeezing the buck until the eagle grins. This is where we come from. We forgot."

Vicki Robin, who has been called one of the Gurus of the New Frugality, believes that frugality will be a major social trend in the nineties. She says that for many aging baby boomers it's a matter of placing more value on time than money, more on family than career. Many of these baby boomers made the big bucks and spent them, only to find that possessions didn't make them happy. Robin suggests that others never achieved the Madison Avenue ideal of consumerism, and they are fast losing hope that they ever will. Frugality is a useful philosophical adjustment for reduced expectations. For many people, it's a simple case of maturity. Young people, flush with the newfound power of a paycheck, often feel they have their entire lives to make up for the money they're about to merrily squander. Somehow after age thirty, visions of mortality and meager retirement benefits start to crowd them with very uneasy feelings. They start to understand that security can vanish overnight. All you have to do is read the newspaper to realize there is no security in your jobs anymore.

I strongly suggest that your goal be *conscious spending*, not deprivation. Instead of measuring purchases strictly by the dollar, also consider how much time, or life energy you lose on the *earn-and-spend treadmill*! It's time to stop living the old, outmoded traditions and create an entirely new concept for success. Recently, I met a financial planner who told me a story that demonstrates what I am saying here.

A young, highly successful couple had recently sought his advice. The husband was a doctor, the wife in sales, and between them they made a healthy six-figure income.

They owned a huge house in the very best part of town, fully equipped with all the "necessary" status extras: pool, gardens, and the full staff needed to maintain them; and they even had country club memberships. Sounds enviable, but in truth, they were miserable.

It seems they really never got to enjoy any of their luxuries because they both had to work sixty to seventy-five hours a week to keep up with the payments, maintenance, and insurance on their possessions! They had all the trappings of wealth but in reality never had time to enjoy them. They spent so much on their life style that they had no savings or other investments and no time or money left over for vacations. Instead of owning their house, it was owning them. Instead of living for themselves, they were living for others and ruining their marriage in the process, to maintain an image for the world that was nothing more than an empty illusion of prosperity. In fact, they had come to the financial planner for advice because their marriage was in trouble, since they also didn't have time for each other. They knew that, if something didn't change quickly, they might lose not only their relationship, but everything they worked for together.

The first thing the financial planner did was to have them redefine the things they owned in terms of "hours of work" spent paying for them, instead of monetary terms. To do this he asked them to figure out how many hours they really worked per month, and then to divide that number of hours into their monthly income. They then evaluated each item they owned or were paying for in these new terms. This clarified their position in a very bright, harsh spotlight for them. When they did this exercise, it did not take long for reality to catch up, showing them how they were no longer working for themselves, but for their possessions. In this new light, they were able to see they had no real prosperity by our new definition, for they were unable to enjoy the fruits of their own labors. They certainly were not at peace with themselves, and they did not feel fulfilled. When the couple returned with the figures in hand, they brought with them an important realization.

It was past time for them to make a change; the life that they had created was not bringing them joy. Once they saw things through this new perspective, they chose to rearrange their lives. They sold the huge home and moved to a smaller one that didn't require so much time, energy, and money to maintain. This new house was still a nice home but, more than that, it was now one they would have time to enjoy, instead of one that would impress others. They trimmed down both their possessions and debts to a manageable level. They got rid of status symbols such as the country club memberships they used only a few times a year. They were both able to scale down their workloads and began to spend quality time together cooking, traveling, and simply enjoying each other's company. In short, they began doing all the things they said they would do when they had the money, but in reality never did because they never had the time.

Six months later, the couple reported that they were working to become free of debt and were actually baffled as to why they had not made the changes years before. Due to the dramatic reduction in overhead, they were both able to scale down their workloads and thus finally had the free time and the feeling of the good life.

Have you ever felt that you too were caught up in the same or a similar "illusion" of the good life? In truth, it's hard not to be when everywhere we look— on television, in magazines and newspapers, everywhere—we're bombarded with images of laughing, seemingly happy people in expensive cars and beautiful homes, wearing gorgeous clothes. We are led to believe that having more is the answer to being happy. But human nature doesn't work that way.

I have often laughed at myself when I realized that the greatest pleasure I've gotten from most of the cars I dreamt of owning was experienced before I actually picked them up from the showroom. This is true for many of us. As soon as we finally get the object of our desire, we eventually lose interest because we discover that it really doesn't change anything except to add to our debt. In fact, more possessions simply make life more complex. Think about it in these terms for a moment—more material possessions means more stress from accumulated debt and more energy consumed in maintaining your possessions. In reality, you become possessed by your possessions.

I would ask you to think about the things that own you. How many useless things have you bought out of boredom, or in the pretense you were nurturing yourself in buying these things? Madison Avenue is always in the background sending clear messages for you to buy, saying "Go ahead, you're worth it. You deserve it. Go for the gusto—after all you only go around once." What did those items really cost you in terms of stress, lack of time off, or the inability to afford other more meaningful things?

This reassessment is simply a matter of defining for yourself what wealth really means to you and then taking a conscious look at whether you've been living by your own definition or by the media's advertised image. It requires you to make a conscious decision about how you use your resources instead of allowing yourself to fritter them away with no clear goal or direction. By reassessing your life's resources you need to write down your dreams and goals and then create priorities. If, in actuality, a vacation is more important to you than eating out three times a week, you need to be aware of that. Make the decision before the fact, not after you've spent your vacation money by eating out.

To live powerfully is to live consciously. Most people drift through life trying to find happiness in material objects, buying themselves into debt because they actually believe Madison Avenue's jingle that happiness is just around the corner if only they buy the latest product. Become a person of power, recognizing that you must live life from your own values and setting your own course in life.

You can create exactly what you want in life, but you must first know precisely what that is. Arriving at true prosperity is no different than arriving at any other destination. If you were going on a trip, you would know your destination and, before setting out, determine the safest, quickest route to get there. In other words, you would simply plan before you took action. We should follow this same procedure as we travel the road to prosperity and success. In doing so, we insure that we will reach our destination and not become lost on some side road on the way. To achieve prosperity, you must carefully examine your present use of the resources you have. Money is not your only resource; you also have your time, talent, skills, experience, vitality, and life energy. Before you spend your resources in any way, make sure you are receiving fair exchange for value.

I have to confess that I am speaking from experience here, because I've had to work on this new awareness myself. You see, I have an expensive habit that I know I share with many other people. I love shopping and buying beautiful things. Although financial security and a debt-free future is my first priority, my shopping habit used to consume much of my extra income. I found, as I became increasingly successful, that I was working very hard to increase what was fast becoming a lot of expensive clutter in my life. In order to indulge my shopping habit, which I considered both entertaining and therapeutic, I was buying new clothes before I'd gotten wear out of the ones I had already. I found myself buying new outfits when I had clothes in my closet with price tags still on them!

I was getting pleasure from the shopping, but I was also creating huge bills for things I really didn't need. This caused a great deal of stress in both my inner and outer life, drawing me away from my true goal. I didn't particularly want to give up my shopping habit, for having money to buy beautiful things was part of my definition of prosperity. I adored browsing through art shows and finding lovely creations. Yet, something was amiss, for I was paying too highly for this pleasure, and not getting real use or value out of what I bought. I realized that in this area I was squandering my hard-earned resources of time and money.

I decided to apply this same maxim I've just been teaching you to myself. I decided to make my habit support me, instead of me supporting it. Since I did enjoy shopping,

I shifted my focus from buying things I really didn't need for myself to buying things I ultimately would need such as gifts for others for Christmas, birthdays, etc. In doing so, I retained the pleasure of browsing and finding great buys, but now I really used what I purchased in a constructive way, a way that not only brought pleasure to myself but to others as well.

This new approach actually began saving me money because it eliminated all my impulse gift buying. No more last minute purchases that caused me to spend twice as much as I intended; with my new strategy I was always prepared. Of course, I still got the fun of shopping, only now I was actually saving money which I could spend in more meaningful ways, perhaps on a super vacation, or prepaying mortgage payments on my home. I merely redefined my viewpoint about "wealth" and began to simplify my life. Now, instead of paying outrageous bills at the end of each month for all the clutter that was expending so much of my time, I had money left in reserve should something unexpected happen. I felt more in control of my life. What I did is to simply create a strategy to bring more balance into my life—balancing impulsive desires with real needs. I took my spending out of the realm of an unconscious habit and made conscious self-empowering decisions concerning it. I became the master of my spending, instead of it being mine.

You see, redefining prosperity doesn't demand deprivation; it only demands we prioritize our dreams and eliminate our waste. We are now living in a time where awareness of proper use of our resources is of the utmost importance. This is reflected to us not only on an individual level, but on a national and global level as well. Our security rests not only in our ability to generate funds, but in the proper guardianship of those funds once we have obtained them. There is one truth you must always remember—there is no security in life except the security that you create for yourself.

I cannot define your personal concept of prosperity for you, but I can tell you that until you have defined it for yourself, you will never have the possibility of achieving it. Until you know what really defines both inner and outer wealth to you, your possessions will own you, instead of the other way around. In today's high-stress world we must reverse the old saying that "time is money," and recognize that "money is time." Each of us has only 1,440 minutes per day to spend; it's up to us to make sure our choices are those that serve us in the fullness of our lives. The only way to learn about your spending behavior is to keep track of every dollar that passes through your hands.

Reassess Your Prosperity

From personal experience, I know that if you don't take the time to keep track of your resources (remember that we're talking about time here as well as money), and write down everything, you won't get a clear picture of what you spend or how you spend it. The illusion of how you spend your time and money is probably very different from how you actually spend it. You will likely be shocked to learn how much you spend on small, insignificant events or purchases. You may well nickel-and-dime yourself to death with no real value to show for your money.

Create a daily money log with categories set up that reflect your spending habits. This is not an accounting exercise; it's a process to help you discover exactly what value you are receiving for your time, energy, and money. Please make your categories as specific as possible. For example, make a category for eating out, then one category for food at home, and another for lunches and snacks at work. The energy you expend to complete this daily log will give you some very surprising answers on where all your extra time and money goes. But knowing this information isn't enough. You must now start thinking about what you're getting for your money. Was it worth the time spent to earn the money to pay for the life style you are living?

Formula for a Personal Accounting Inventory

1. Invest in an accounting journal.
2. List in detail all your bills and monthly expenses.

3. List your income and divide your income by the number of hours you work each month.
4. Detail how many hours, days or weeks, you have to work to simply cover your monthly expenses.
5. Determine how much money is left after paying all your monthly bills.
6. Make a plan for how to use your extra income to become debt-free.
7. Create a realistic budget, one that includes money allotted for necessities and money to save or invest.

To determine how efficiently you've been spending your money, recall the last ten items on which you spent $50 or more and ask yourself these questions:

1. What value did this item bring?
2. Could I have used that money more resourcefully?

Before making future non-necessity purchases, ask yourself these questions:

1. How many hours do I have to work to pay for this item?
2. How many hours of use or pleasure will I receive from this?
3. In six months will I still find this item attractive?
4. Is there something else I want more than this item?

If all your answers are favorable, then by all means, invest and enjoy. But when using this acid test, if this expenditure will not still be attractive to you in six months, hold off and invest your money in ways that will create a better return for your money and effort.

I personally see the future as an exciting time. I am choosing to use my resources in more productive ways. Since life is exactly how you decide to look at it, you are the writer of the movie of your life. If you look upon making these changes as difficult or burdensome, then you will suffer because they will indeed be just that. However, if you choose to see the creative challenge and excitement of changing your life strategies, you will create the prosperity consciousness attitude and progress toward a more debt-free life.

Answer the following questions as truthfully as possible to motivate you to make some changes in the way you see and experience wealth.

1. What will your future look like in five years if you continue your same spending patterns?
2. What would your life be like if you weren't burdened by debt?
3. Are you an impulse buyer?
4. Instead of buying new things, what other ways could you use your energy to create pleasure in your life?
5. How much could you save to create security for yourself if you created and lived within a budget?

Anyone can be wasteful with money and resources. It takes no real talent or creativity to do so, for it is programming we've received from the advertising media all our life. Creating a rich, fulfilling, meaningful life, which abounds with the things and activities you value personally, takes thorough creativity and self-discipline. It requires believing in your own power to become the master of both your inner and outer worlds.

_12_
HOW TO PLUG ENERGY LEAKS
THAT HOLD YOU BACK FROM SUCCESS

It's not that we all don't have great ideas, projects we want to get done, people we want to help; the problem is that we have no energy to do the extra things in life that we would like to do. We, as human beings, have only so much life energy we can use in any given day. Our lives are changing at a rapid pace and it feels as if we have too many people, responsibilities, necessities, pulling us in a thousand different directions every waking hour. It's no surprise that we feel stressed out and and fatigued.

The problem isn't just our life style; it's also how we use our existing life energy. We all have something I call energy leaks. Those self-defeating behaviors that drain our energy by creating anxiety. Energy leaks occur when we use our mental or emotional energy on our thoughts, worries, doubts, fears, and grudges. When we cannot maintain our energy level, we cannot learn new skills, adapt to new procedures, and assimilate changing directions.

The purpose of this chapter is to make you aware of the unconscious energy leaks that can influence the overall quality of your life as well as strategies to use your life energy more effectively.

An energy leak that almost everyone has is wasting life by trying to live in the past or the future. How many times have you caught yourself saying things like: *I can't wait till 5 o'clock, I can't wait 'till Friday, 'till my vacation, 'till I get married, 'till the kids get in school?* When we daydream of the future or spend a lot of time comparing how the past was better, we are actually stealing from our current life energy to be in the present.

Have you ever caught yourself thinking: *Things used to be so much better; being a kid was so great, when I was younger?* The problem in doing this is that you're stealing from the one true resource that can't be replaced—NOW. All you have is this moment in time. Our present time is so precious, yet we act as if it were okay to waste the only thing you really own in life: the present.

You can prevent energy leaks by looking at time from a different perspective. Most of us subscribe to the continuum view of time, which is a useful way of organizing your memories. Remember that your memories are all thought forms, a way of representing our lives. If I were to ask you what the past and future meant to you, you would most likely describe any number of things that have happened to you—some good, some bad—and you would call these experiences your past.

Our past is the present memories of activities, events, people, places, and things. It is also our perceptions and interpretations, combined with our physical and emotional reactions to these things. All of our memories occur in the present time—all you have in life is the present. The past is a locked door; we cannot go back and change anything.

When you describe the future, you will most likely talk about events that may happen. What we like to call the future is really the use of our imagination. We base our future on the memories of the past, just rearranged to meet our expectations of what we think the future will be like.

A wonderful description of wasting your life by not living in the present is found in Scott Morrison's book, *From Open and Innocent: The Gentle and Passionate Art of Not Knowing.*

He writes,

> The problem is that even if we are intellectually understanding that time is fictitious, that this present is all that we ever have, have had or ever will have. For if we proceed to live as if the past and future are not only separate, actual times, but somehow, more important than the present, then we deprive our-

selves of awareness of the only moment we can ever enjoy anything, the only time we can ever truly know peace, joy, love, freedom, happiness, wisdom, compassion—the very things we say our lives are about.

Furthermore, when we spend our time regretting or longing for the past, or worrying about or long for something in the future, we find we have created problems that have no solutions. Because they are based on remembered or imagined situations, we have no way of doing anything about them. If, however, I realize that the problem is not with the hurts I suffered in childhood (those are over), but rather with my present experience of (and fear of facing) those unresolved and very real present memories of pain, embarrassment, humiliation or terror stored in my mind and body now, then I suddenly realize I have a clear choice as to whether I will assume responsibility for my own healing or not.

In regard to future concerns, if I realize that the process of worrying about not being able to pay my bills next month or losing my relationship or not getting something I regard as important (those things haven't happened yet) is basically a waste of energy, then I am freed up to enjoy and do and be whatever is here and necessary right now. I find I can actually live my life rather than just thinking or worrying about it.

Your time and energy should be at the top of your list of most precious resources. It's the steps you take in the present which will allow you to manifest whatever it is that you want in your future. The bottom line is *your point of power is always in the present.*

For example, if you have children, think about how often you're at work and your efficiency is suddenly paralyzed because of a phone call from one of your kids. You begin to feel guilty about being away from them and berate yourself with how you're not a good parent because you work so many hours. Then you go home and, while you're with your family, begin to feel guilty and worry about the work left unfinished.

Many of us can relate to this scenario and are losing

out on both sides. Your creative and productive energy is being wasted at work because you're focused on not being a good parent. At home your mind is back at work causing you to miss out on enjoying your family time. This is a major energy leak in life resulting in frustration. You end up creating a situation where you aren't living in the present moment.

One very effective way to learn to be in control, to minimize or even stop energy leaks, is to divide your life into compartments. When you're at work, leave your personal worries at home; you can be assured that they will be there when you get back. One of the great advantages to leaving your personal problems at home is that it allows you to focus your attention on your work, where it goes without saying you will be much more productive and less stressed out. Another upside of leaving your personal problems at home is that your mind gets a well-deserved rest.

When you stop actively thinking about your problems, your subconscious mind has the opportunity to search through its many knowledge files of your past experiences to look for a workable solution. The more you worry and fret over your problems, the more unresourceful you will become. Stuck in the same old mindset, you cannot see what other potential opportunities may exist for solving your problem. By simply letting the problem go for a few hours you actually improve your chances for coming up with workable solutions.

The same holds true for any type of problem, personal or business. You need to give your computer the opportunity to offer additional options. When you refocus on the problem you will be able to analyze it from a different perspective. This new viewpoint allows you to see new strategies to use. The following paragraphs offer some popular examples of energy leaks.

Home Energy Conservation

To plug an energy leak at home, just keep in mind one important fact—your employer does not pay you enough to take your business problems home—leave them at work.

When you get home, give yourself permission to be in the present and let your personal life be separate from your work life.

Random Preoccupation

Being preoccupied twenty-four hours a day with thinking about your work or personal problems means you have a one-track mind which will leave you no energy to develop other areas of interests or recognize and enjoy the blessings in your life. Television newswoman Barbara Walters interviewed the famous director John Huston before he passed away and asked him what was most important in life: money, fame, or power? He replied that none of those things were important for him. He felt the most important thing in life was outside interests, keeping your mind open to learn about new things. The spark of life is having the energy to enjoy many things.

Nag, Nag, Nag

If you have nagging thoughts, you're supporting all that information in your mind which, just like a computer, has only so much room for storage of information; you leave yourself no room for the interests or pleasures you want to experience.

Let's Do Lunch

Another source of energy leaks are insincere commitments such as the phrase "Oh, I would love to (you fill in the obligation)—call me." If you know in your heart that don't want to do that something, stop playing games with your mind and your time. Learn to say "No" with love and kindness. It takes much less energy than thinking of an excuse the sixth time the person calls you to fulfill your social obligation!

Skeletons In The Closet

If you are like millions of other human beings (with the exception of movie star George Hamilton who, according to television show "Life Styles of the Rich and Famous" has his closet fully cross-referenced and automated), your closet probably represents a full-fledged energy crisis. You would expend less energy simply organizing the chaos— donating unused and unwanted items or mending needed repairs to items you like—than you spend worrying about what to wear!

Excess Baggage

A most damaging energy leak is holding on to angry feelings—bearing a grudge. As an example, Tammy is a friend of mine; she and her husband had just moved into their first home when she found out she was expecting their first child. The new house needed a complete paint job so Tammy's father offered to come over and help her paint. After two weeks of hard work in close quarters, Tammy and her father began to get on each other's nerves. One day they had a raging fight where both of them said some very nasty things to each other. Her father ultimately left the house angry and refused to come back and finish painting. They haven't spoken to each other since the big blowup, leaving Tammy so upset that she bursts into tears at the mere thought of her father. Tammy's husband wants her to call her father for a reconciliation, but she remains adamant that it's his place to call her. After all, she is expecting her first child and he deserted her in the middle of this huge painting job, even though she recognizes the blow up was really over a misunderstanding and nothing to argue about. She stubbornly maintains that she is right. The problem here is that she would rather be right than have peace in her family—and this energy leak of worrying about the rift in her family is creating unhappiness for her.

No matter who you are, you have some type of similar story from your own life. So many times, we hold on to our righteous feelings, even when it hurts us. We are too stubborn to give in and admit that we are 50 percent of the problem. The amount of life energy that is consumed by clinging to who is right drains us from seeing other solutions and reconciling with the people we care about.

Worry Leaks

Worry is a useless emotion. Since your brain doesn't have enough information to worry accurately, you're making it up, and most likely, it's 100 percent worse than reality could ever be. If you have unhealthy emotions of imagined fears or worry, the body responds with a tense feeling of nervousness, stress-related illness, fatigue, lack of energy, and loss of creativity. Ever heard this saying—"the fearful die a thousand deaths, the brave only one"? When you live under fear of what might happen, you are so physically exhausted that you are unable to be creative and cope with normal challenges or emergencies that might happen. Make a vow to yourself today to cross a bridge only as you come to it.

You must take back your power in life by staying in the present and dealing with the realities. You are not a victim of circumstance; you make your own internal environment. You are the creator of your life by your thoughts and actions. Your subconscious mind will produce whatever you ask for; just as a computer doesn't care what information you put in, it will act on that information. We must stop letting worry control us.

Samuel Johnson observed: "The fountain of content must spring up in the mind, and he who hath so little knowledge of human nature as to seek happiness by changing anything but his own disposition, will waste his life in fruitless efforts and multiply the grief he proposes to remove."

Guilt Leaks

Our society has conditioned us to feel guilty. It's a learned emotional response. We have been taught to believe that if you feel guilty it shows that you're a good person who cares. Guilt is a neurotic behavior that our society has come to accept as normal. It has nothing to do with caring. It's pure manipulation to control other people. Since the pain of guilt makes us feel so bad, we will do just about anything to please others so we do not have to feel guilty.

By feeling guilty in an attempt to show that we are sorry for our actions and really care, we are in reality simply getting into a very unresourceful state of mind and beating ourselves up in an attempt to change what is now history. The past is a locked door and whatever occurred cannot be changed. Your regret doesn't make things any better. Feeling guilty has never fixed any problem. Guilt simply holds you prisoner of the past and immobilizes you from taking resourceful action in the present. The more you dwell in the guilty state of mind, the less creative you can be in dealing with your responsibilities of the present. Now is all you have in life—the future is created by the choices and steps you take today.

We choose how to use our life energy. To really be a fully functioning person, you must learn from the past, not whip yourself because of it. Mistakes should be treated like a speck of dust in the eye: you identify the problem; instead of condemning yourself or feeling guilty for having it, you quite simply just get rid of it. The sooner you do, the sooner you will be free from the problem.

STRATEGIES TO PLUG THOSE ENERGY LEAKS

Grudge Release Levers

Many people ask how it could be in our best interest to forgive someone who has betrayed, humiliated, abused, or rejected us? Over the centuries, religious leaders have counseled us to turn the other cheek; today's mental health professionals emphasize that forgiveness implies that you're responsible for your own emotional needs.

Since you only have so much mental, physical, spiritual, and emotional life energy, if you spend it holding on to negative or angry feelings, whom do you really hurt? Yourself, of course. When you are plotting revenge, going over what you would like to say in your mind, you drain positive creative energy that could be used in a more resourceful way, such as getting some projects done or having fun. You never hurt the person you are holding the grudge against. You end up hurting only yourself because of the time and energy wasted.

Food for thought—is it possible to reframe this situation

in your mind? Remembering that people do the best they can with the knowledge they have, you can choose to forgive them. That doesn't mean you agree with what they did. Maybe the bottom line is that they didn't really mean to hurt you. According to Sidney and Suzanne Simon's book, *Forgiveness: How to Make Peace with Your Past and Get on with Your Life*, "Forgiveness is a by-product of a long process of healing, and only after you acknowledge, work through, and let go of hurt can you lead a full life." They went on to say, "Forgiveness doesn't mean condoning what someone did, or forgetting it, or absolving that person from responsibility. Forgiveness doesn't mean they get off scot-free. It means you get off scot-free, you do it for yourself."

To forgive someone doesn't mean you have to write or call or even go to see them. All you have to do is forgive and release them in your mind. Every time you think of that person, do a pattern-interrupt on yourself and say to yourself that you forgive and release them and then send them positive thoughts. The advantage of using this type of approach is that the next time you see them or someone else brings up their name, you'll no longer have that negative emotional reaction. You've raised your standards of living and given yourself the leverage to create emotional management for yourself; you achieve this by forgiving them and letting go of the emotional baggage you've been carrying that needlessly drains you of energy.

According to mental-health professionals, taking responsibility for your own feelings by choosing to forgive can boost your self-esteem and your ability to feel in control of your destiny. Studies have shown that when people are able to forgive and let go of their hurt and/or anger, it can open the way to resolving seemingly unconnected problems such as compulsive overeating, drugs, alcohol abuse, and depression. You have everything to gain and nothing to lose but self-pity, anger, and resentment if you give yourself permission to forgive and release. Being 100 percent responsible for yourself extracts you from the perspective of being a victim. The act of forgiveness gives *you* the piece of mind. I love the old saying, The best revenge is living well!

Forgive Yourself

We are really toughest on ourselves and usually expect to be perfect. If you live your present life by comparing yourself to the mistakes of the past, you only undermine your confidence level. What you focus on expands for you. If you focus on and relive your mistakes or failures, you are simply reinforcing why you can not succeed in the present. *Never reinforce the negative!* Instead, spend your life energy focusing on what you can do.

Everyone has a few skeletons in their closets. When I look back on some of my mistakes, recalling the times I've hurt people and said or done the wrong thing, I have to acknowledge that I was doing the best I could at the time with my knowledge, skills, and resources. It's clear I made mistakes, but I can't continue beating myself up in the present, futilely attempting to change history with my bad feelings or guilt. I must have the courage to face myself, accept the learning experience, and *move on*. I also want to remind you that your entire life will be a matter of making mistakes and failing from time to time. The point is to forgive yourself, learn the valuable information, and *move on*. This one act of releasing the past and not letting it use up any more of your life energy will free you to be more at peace with yourself. Releasing that stored-up negative energy that has been clogging up your system will open your creative channels of energy to become more productive.

Productivity Lists

List making is an excellent way to avoid energy leaks. Once you write something down, it's firmly imprinted on your mental computer. The most important reason for creating a list is that it simply allows you to organize your thoughts and you no longer have to use mental energy to think about it. I keep a running "To Do" list and prioritize it with four columns: A—Must Do, B—Want To Do, C—Will Do If I Have Time, D—Delegate It! The list keeps me from having to hold the information in my mind. Even if you lose the list, you are more likely to remember what it is you needed to do or buy because you wrote it down.

Skill Of Awareness

One of the most effective ways to stop your energy leaks is to first acknowledge a distraction in your mind and to realize you are not living in your present. You then have a choice: succumb to the wandering of your mind or take control of your thoughts and redirect your focus. As an example, you're at a party that you're not really enjoying because you're thinking you should be home finishing a report for work. I speak with authority on this example; when I realize I'm not enjoying the present moment because of distracting thoughts, I use what I call the Scarlet O'Hara technique—tell myself I'll think about or solve this problem tomorrow. Then I use a short mental exercise to bring my attention and awareness back to the present.

I imagine in my mind a large storage chest. I see myself opening this big oversized trunk and putting all my to-do lists, worries, fears, and guilty feelings in it for safekeeping when I close and lock the trunk shut. Then I release the mental image and tune into the present. I have personally found this mental exercise to be very beneficial because it allows me to let go of my energy leaks for the moment. I have satisfied myself with putting those thoughts in a safe place where I can return to deal with them later.

A Job Well Done (Finally!)

One of the energy drains I frequently experience is the frustration of not being able to complete as many things each day as I would like. If your life is like mine, you have dozens of projects every week and most of these projects are on-going issues. Lingering tasks or projects can unfortunately leave you frustrated, lacking that sense of completion. Even small projects give you a sense of accomplishment when you complete them. One of the strategies I use and highly recommend is to allow yourself fifteen to thirty minutes each day to do some type of task that will give you a sense of accomplishment and completion.

For example, in my office or home there is always a drawer, closet, or area that needs to be cleaned out and organized. You probably have one too. This is an energy drain because, every time you go this location, your brain gnaws at you reminding you, *This needs to be cleaned out, organized, etc.* Allowing yourself the fifteen to thirty minutes a day to tackle that small task will give you a sense of pride and accomplishment when you are finished. It's important that we reward ourselves with these small victories. Take your opportunities to turn an energy leak into an energy boost! Since I started this one-small-project-a-day routine, I've noticed that many of my energy drains are now gone. This is simply because I've allowed myself to look at my long-term intentions and invested a small amount of time and energy to take care of the leak.

News At A Later Date

Another important strategy for dealing with energy leaks is taking charge of the caliber of information that goes into your mind. On an average day—when you turn on your radio or television or read your newspaper—you get a gloom-and-doom diet of world events. In effect, you are being programmed by the media: crime is up, education is down, the quality of our life is deteriorating, natural disasters and widespread death are raging, there is an alternating possibility of war and the apparent destruction of our planet—not even considering what the economic indicators are saying about the economy! All this negative information eventually weighs down our minds, eroding on our confidence. Our creative life energy is being used up by worry and fear of our future's outlook.

I challenge you to a very drastic measure. For the next 21 days, cancel your newspaper and stop listening to the radio/television news. Instead of exposing yourself to outside programming that creates fear, doubt, and hopelessness, substitute any type of positive, educational, or inspiring information in its place. There are so many self-help books and motivational audio tapes available to charge up your day. I'm not suggesting that on a long-term basis you stick your head in the sand and not pay any attention to the news or what is going on in the world; I'm not suggesting that you stop caring about other people or not deal with reality. What I am suggesting is to implement some energy plugs. You take control of your life by taking control of the caliber of information that goes into your computer—your brain.

On a daily basis we allow this energy drain of negative news reports to affect our attitude and our motivation without recognizing the source. If you're feeling disheartened and hopelessly out of control after a morning's dose of discouraging news, you will most likely not be able to muster the mental, physical, or emotional life energy you need to be creative and deal effectively with the change and uncertainty of everyday life.

The first couple of days of using this strategy of not reading or hearing about the daily news, you may have symptoms of withdrawal. However, you will start waking up feeling more excited and optimistic about your day. Substituting inspirational reading material for the newspaper allows you to be more productive and less distracted by the daily news. You will no longer be frightened by the world and disheartened by its troubles. Instead of depleting your energy first thing in the morning, you will be charging yourself up with empowering information.

Leaks Of Indecisiveness

No decision *is* a decision. It's a decision of default. It's allowing the circumstances of your life to dictate your direction. It is said that lack of decision heads the list of major reasons for failure. Since your brain is a computer, it needs a clear and specific direction to be able to give you options and solutions. If you don't guide your brain with what you're expecting from a decision, it cannot give you resourceful information.

When you are faced with the task of making an important decision, you can use several techniques. First, to clarify the problem, write it out on paper; then create two columns to weigh all the potential positive and negative results you might receive contingent on how you make the decision.

You can go to a very private and quiet place where you can focus on the situation. Then write down everything you have to gain in one column and everything you have to lose in the next.

By the time you've listed the pros and cons, it will be crystal clear as to which column holds the strongest evidence to act on. This systematic analysis helps to organize your feelings and priorities allowing you to arrive at a logical decision.

You should also look into the future with your mind. Ask yourself this important, risk-bearing question: What is the worst thing that could happen because of my decision? It's important to weigh all the possibilities before proceeding with the decision. The reason you want to look at the possible downsides is because you have to ask yourself one more important question: Can you live with this possibility? If not, maybe you shouldn't risk it—all risks should be carefully considered in your mind for all possible outcomes.

Here is an example from my own life. After I had been in business for myself as a professional speaker for two years, the recession was still raging, and as a new business, I was not able to support myself yet solely as a speaker. I realized I must become more versatile to earn an income if I were going to survive in my new-found profession. I had been urged by several of my dearest friends and business associates that I should be pursuing work in the television industry.

Finally, I seriously considered the pros and cons of trying to get into television. I looked at my worst case of what could happen if I tried—that was that I would be rejected by everyone in the industry! Another big downside is what the effort would cost me in time and money invested as well as the lack of income I could be earning if I were working on my business as a speaker.

After weighing all the possibilities, I decided that I could live with the rejection if it came. It may not feel inspiring, but it's never been proven to be fatal!

The benefits of making the decision to start working in television far outweighed the potential negative effects. Whenever making an important decision, always listen to your gut feeling about the decision. When "things feel wrong," hold off making a decision and honor your sixth sense. Give yourself time to do additional research. If the decision "feels wrong" analyze your options of putting off the decision—more often than not you've got little to lose by giving yourself a little more time which could save you much more in the long run. But if it feels right, trust yourself and take action.

CHAPTER
_13_
FACE YOUR DRAGONS
AND WIN THE GAME OF LIFE

Our emotions drive our lives. Acknowledging information in your mind will not always connect with your emotions. We all know that we have dreams and goals that would make our lives more exciting, but we stop ourselves from reaching for these dreams. Instead we give ourselves reasons why we will fail: others will not approve, or we just will not be good enough. We are all consciously and unconsciously giving away our personal power and life energy to what I call Life Dragons.

Our dragons are insecurities that we are not good enough, smart enough, attractive enough, young or old enough to do whatever it is we want to do. We have let these dragons become so large in our minds that we feel powerless against them. Negative self-talk has reinforced our rationale for why we won't go for something we want. We start to program ourselves to fail; what's the use of trying anyway—we already know we'll fail. We build such a strong case against ourselves that we lose our creative energy to take the first step. We avoid what we fear we may not be able to do with perfection. Our efforts have become shrouded in frustration and we lose our sense of certainty—that winning edge.

As a self-fulfilling prophecy, our focus always becomes our reality. We do have the power within us to refocus our energy and thoughts, create new solutions, give ourselves more leverage, and overcome outdated fears that hold us back from creating a satisfying life. When you look back in your own history you can clearly see that fighting imaginary dragons is a waste of your life energy and time. It's while you are battling a dragon that you don't see what alternatives you have; most of us feel trapped and cornered. Dragons or fears that have not been faced will have many long-ranging, negative effects on your life today and your future successes.

One unusually warm night in April, restless and unable to sleep, I climbed out of bed to sit on my porch overlooking the Chesapeake Bay—suddenly overwhelmed with the distinct feeling that I must again begin the book. Two years earlier, acting on the advice of my booking agent and several of my colleagues, I'd begun to attempt to write my first book alone—a career move that I was told would take me to the next level in my profession. Little did I know that what followed would be one of the most profound lessons of my life—one that would cost me untold time, energy and money and would once and for all wake me to the importance of listening to my own inner voice. The project began in May of 1990, and after twenty grueling months of working with a host of different ghost writers—all who had their own ideas about what I should say and how I should say it—I simply gave up. They couldn't climb inside in my head to say what only I could say, and I did not yet have the courage to dig down deep enough to write it myself.

But that night in April, something changed. It was as if I felt a nudge from inside. Was I really going to let a mere book get the best of me? After all, I had always taken pride in the fact that I wasn't one to give up easily. No matter what, I always had perseverance. Yet, faced with the momentous task of writing a book, I turned into a quivering mass of fears and insecurities. Quite simply, I just didn't believe I had what it took to write a book. Yet since two months earlier, when I had abandoned the idea altogether, not a single day had passed that I hadn't questioned the decision. That night I suddenly saw the truth for the first time—I simply wasn't willing to let it go.

From that night forward something shifted inside me. I just knew—no matter what—I must write the book. But this time it wasn't for my career, or fame, or to impress my colleagues; this time I would write it because I had something important to say.

This is just one experience of many where, as I look back on my life, I realize that I have created so much more pain while trying to avoid the imagined pain. With the skill of awareness, we all have the power and courage to look our dragons in the eye and know that if you give yourself permission you can deal with any problem or situation. The price for not facing your dragons is lost opportunities, time, self-esteem, and misuse of potential and talent. Frankly, I've grown to believe it's easier to face up to life and do the best you can—not to let fear and doubt rule my life.

Have Courage

We are all bombarded by fears, doubts, and reasons why we cannot accomplish what we want for ourselves; to help put things into perspective, let me give you an interesting definition of the word fear: *Fantasized Experiences Appearing Real.* Most of the things we fear are simply an exaggeration of our imagination. Since our subconscious mind and our nervous system doesn't know the difference between reality and our imagination, it produces the same uncomfortable feelings of anxiety. Our self-talk has created dragons that appear too big for us to handle.

You must allow yourself to experience your fears and move through them with courage—the courage to look, acknowledge, and experience. Don't resist, avoid, or condemn your fears. It's an interesting paradox in life that when you resist something it persists. Allowing yourself this growth process is like a butterfly freeing itself from the cocoon. Many famous writers and artists alike recognize the importance of this metamorphosis. Ralph Waldo Emerson said, "Do the thing you fear and the death of fear is certain." Eleanor Roosevelt observed, "You gain strength, courage and confidence by every experience in which you must stop and look fear in the face. You must do the thing you think you cannot do." And Mark Twain put it this way: "Courage is resistance to fear, mastery of fear—not absence of fear." The truth is that success is never final and failure is never fatal—it's courage that counts.

Be an Effective Risk Taker

Progress in life is always going to involve risk. Many of us are afraid at the mention of the word because we associate pain with risk. In reality, for you to be in control of your own destiny, you must be willing to be an actor in life versus a reactor to life. This means you must be willing to risk failure in order to grow. People who make no mistakes usually don't take any risks and therefore never allow themselves any opportunity to stretch and grow using their potential. In our past programming, many of us have been taught to play it safe, to not risk trying something new. We create an abundance of opportunities by trying new experiences. Every experience gives you additional resources and teaches you valuable information from which to draw. You have to look at life from a point of view where there is no such thing as failure, only results. For every adversity, there is an opportunity to learn.

A supreme example of adversity in my own life happened when I was working with a large booking agency in Canada that had been promoting me in public seminars for over three years. This booking agency had spent a tremendous amount of time and money creating a good public persona for me. Throughout the final year I worked as a subcontractor with them, I noticed there had been a change in their behavior and they weren't paying for my speaking services on time. Because I considered them friends as well as business associates, I allowed them become very delinquent in paying me a significant amount of money. After all, they had been successful in promoting my human potential seminars, along with many other types of training programs.

To my dismay, I learned that my seminars were the only programs creating any significant profit for the agency. The problem had occurred when they didn't change their business strategy as they started to lose money. Since they hadn't learned from their mistakes, they continued to do things the same way as they had done them for years; only now it wasn't working. Finally one day, to my horror, I received a bankruptcy notice from them.

For about a month I was very depressed and upset not only over the loss of promotion and the source of potential future income, but also for the tremendous amount of money I was already due! I began to realize that I needed to stop blaming them and deal with reality. My future was going to be determined by how resourceful I could now be in spite of external circumstances.

I finally gathered the courage to face this dragon and start to ask myself empowering questions on how to benefit from this situation. I asked myself over and over again throughout every day, *What can I do about this situation? What opportunities are in this setback for me?*

Then finally one day as I stepped into the shower, my intuition gave me the answer. Why not start my own booking agency in Canada and take advantage of the good promotion/public relations efforts of the now-bankrupt company? The end result was that I formed a partnership with one of the former members of the old booking company's staff and we started our own seminar company in Canada. I am grateful for that seemingly negative situation now because without that unfortunate event I would not have had the opportunity to expand into an international market so quickly or form a partnership with another wonderful human being who inspires me to be my best. A quote from General Patton influenced me at the time: "Success is not getting on top—but how you bounce on the bottom that counts."

The most successful men and women in history have all had to deal with change, uncertainty, and fear. The obstacles of your past can become the gateways that lead to new beginnings. It's clear that progress always involves risk. We shouldn't fear trying something new or be afraid if our efforts do not work out, because we will always gain experience and wisdom.

FEARS THAT HOLD US BACK

The Fear-Of-Failure Dragon

Do you know anyone who hasn't failed at something? Most likely not. I have always felt inspired by reading about Walt Disney. Most people don't know that he failed several times. He went broke, was bankrupt, and weathered some really tough times. But he was a visionary. He was willing to learn from his situation, regroup, reevaluate, relearn, and move on. Napoleon Hill, author of *Think & Grow Rich*, said, "If you make a plan and that plan fails, make another plan. If that plan fails make another plan. The only people who fail in life are the ones who give up." Malcom Forbes said, "Failure is success if you learn from it." Henry Ford said, "One who fears failure limits his worth because failure is the opportunity to begin again more intelligently."

The Fear-Of-Making-A-Mistake Dragon

Remember the number-one fear for business people is speaking in front of a group? I think that boils down to the fact that individuals are afraid of standing in front of a group of people and making a mistake.

The only time you really make mistakes in life is if you continue a behavior or a strategy over and over and it doesn't work. The first time you do something wrong is called a learning experience.

IBM founder T.J. Watson said, "It is important to acknowledge a mistake instantly, correct it and learn from it. That literally turns a failure into a success. Success is on the far side of failure."

The Fear-Of-Criticism Dragon

So many times in life we would like to try a new sport, cut our hair in a different way, go into business for ourselves, stand up for our rights, and tell people what we really think. But we're afraid of what criticism we might receive because of our actions. We've been brainwashed that other people's opinions are more important than our own feelings. We don't want to be judged. To take back your life you must not be outer-directed; you must be inner-directed. Whose life is this anyway?

Do these other people walk in your shoes? Do they know what's in your heart? Do they know your needs, desires, and goals? When you hear criticism, listen for the truth. Ask yourself, *Is there any truth in what they are saying? If so, how can I learn or grow from the feedback?* If your intuition tells you that the information is not true, discard it! It's time for us to stop fearing what other people are going to criticize and live our own lives by our own truths—remind yourself of another famous saying, *To Thine Own Self Be True.*

The Perfectionist Dragon

While talking to people over the years, I have noticed one of the most destructive habits you can have is being a perfectionist. Most people don't even realize it, but being a perfectionist creates procrastination—putting off doing what you know needs to be done. At the root of procrastination is a fear that we won't do something perfectly so we are reluctant to get started. A perfectionist is a person who is always looking for something wrong, and who will find it since that is where their focus is. Then the perfectionist is shocked and angry that something or someone is not perfect. To them any flaw means total failure. This type of thinking leaves no middle ground; you're either perfect or a complete failure.

Since little in life is perfect, perfectionists are usually frustrated, angry, and disappointed with life. With their attitude that things must always be perfect, it's difficult for them to accept themselves and others for who they really are. Perfectionists are very critical and judgmental; no one is good enough. These same people look for everything in life to be perfect, fear any type of criticism, and easily become defensive. They cannot bear the thought of being wrong. The attitudes of the perfectionist cause conflicts in all their family, social, and professional relationships. Striving to be perfect creates unrealistic expectations, pressures and problems. Being a perfectionist creates and promotes stress and suffering, while making spontaneity and playfulness almost impossible.

One of the most damaging problems with being a perfectionist is the emphasis on external focus since the emphasis is on such surface qualities as the desire to impress and please others. Perfectionists act as if they think they're supposed to be to be perfect instead of paying attention to the more important inner qualities. The pressures of perfectionist-type thinking holds people back from trying new sports or games, going after a new job, or starting projects.

Again, the root of perfectionist thinking is the false belief that you must be perfect. I've found that there is nothing perfect in life: no perfect careers, marriages, children—in short, no perfect life. So why do we expect ourselves to be perfect? It holds us back from really living!

One of the dragons you can turn your back on is the label of being a perfectionist. Never call yourself that again. It only uses your self-talk to program yourself to look for what is wrong. Instead, label yourself as a person who is flexible. You need to be committed to stretching yourself in life and create a frame of mind of excellence instead of perfectionism, because trying to be perfect creates frustration, whereas striving for excellence means you are being the best you can be. There is an old saying: the person who has given himself the most choices, Wins!

EMPOWERING QUESTIONS TO ASK YOURSELF TO DEFEAT YOUR DRAGONS

Begin by listing your fears, doubts, and insecurities about yourself.

How have your fears and doubts affected your life? Your career? Your income? Your future? Your attitudes? Your abilities?

How much have these dragons cost you in lost income? In upward mobility?

How have your dragons affected your relationships with your family, your children, spouse, friends, and co-workers?

How would your life look different if you were to face your fears and doubts? Now list ten ways your life might be better.

What programming did you get from the past that created your fears?

What has been your strategy to sabotage yourself from trying new things because of your fears?

How do you feel when you stuff your frustration about your fears down inside yourself? How does it show up?

What will your future look like in two years when you face and overcome your dragons?

In what areas of your life are you a perfectionist?

In what areas can you take more effective life risks?

Whose criticism has held you back from trying new things?

_14_
BUILD AN EMOTIONAL FOXHOLE
FOR TOUGH TIMES

Everyone has what I jokingly refer to as character-building days. No matter who you are, you have days you feel overwhelmed by work, the weather, your family, a certain situation, another person, or just life. These days are a fact of living in the real world. No matter how hard you try to be perfect or have a perfect life, there will always be people and events out of your control. Most of the time you can pull yourself up by the bootstraps and deal with the daily challenges that life has to offer you.

However, there are those times that you have to nurture yourself and honor your emotions. Create an emotional foxhole for yourself and retreat from the world for a short time to regroup. Society teaches us that when things go wrong, keep a stiff upper lip, be strong, adopt a don't-let-them-see-you-sweat attitude. Truthfully, this advice can create some long-term emotional problems. We're not taught to honor our own emotional needs. If you go through life blocking or denying the negative feelings you experience, you become numb. When you emotionally shut down or numb out the negative, you also block out the good in your life. Before you know it, you're living in a trance; you walk around unconscious of how you feel.

It's important to grasp the concept that feelings are energy and they need to be acknowledged. The more you deny your feelings the more they will push for recognition. When you decide to take back your life and control your destiny, you must give yourself permission to also accept yourself fully. There is value in understanding that there is an important difference between owning your negative feelings and focusing on them.

When you give yourself permission to own your feelings, you are accepting yourself for what you really feel. It's acceptable to allow yourself to feel helpless, unloved, depressed, lonely, taken advantage of, weak, insecure, afraid, unsure, confused, or lost. Everyone has these feelings from time to time.

By giving yourself permission to acknowledge your feelings, you release some of the internal pressure to be perfect and to be all things to all people. When we deny our emotions and stuff them down inside of us for a long period of time, they build up and start to create bigger problems: mental or physical imbalances such as depression, illness, and anger. By admitting that you have these negative feelings, you allow yourself to release the tension. The problem may still need to be addressed, but much of the pressure and tension has evaporated. You'll be able to arrive at solutions more easily because you're no longer using your energy to deal with your emotions.

I made it a point to interview successful people on what strategies or resources they use when they have a really bad day. One company vice president told me that he knows he is having an emotionally ill day when he feels overwhelmed and beaten up by his job and problems. First, he admits to himself that he needs to get away from it all to regroup. His stress management strategies depend on the time of the year: if it's summer, he goes fishing; if it's winter, he goes home and works in his workshop. The point is that he creates some space for himself to be able to get away from all the phones, bosses, and stressful problems.

By getting away, he can let go and relax. He allows himself to be unproductive and to heal from the hectic activities and pressures. Getting away allows him to listen to himself, to feel bad if he needs to, and to deal with his problems. He stated that he felt men have so much pressure from society to be strong and handle everything perfectly. Allowing downtime for himself allows him to be upset in private. He states that he gives himself a limit of just one day and the next day it's back to the job. Ninety-nine percent of the time, this strategy works for him and keeps him sane. He is currently working on a proposal to his company to make it policy that employees have mental health (or hooky) days to blow off steam and frustrations.

After listening to this executive's story, I had a chance to try out his advice. I experienced firsthand how I had to do more to nurture myself than tell myself to be positive and things would get better in the future. I had just experienced a huge failure in one of my business projects. I was so disappointed with myself in how I had misjudged the situation. It was one of those sure-thing deals where nothing could go wrong. I had worked on perfecting this project for over a year, yet it never got off the ground. I had invested a great deal of my life savings and I fell flat on my face for all the world to see.

I took this failure very personally. My mind was racing on what effect this loss would have on my career and life. I kept thinking: if I had just been better; if I had done things differently; if the economy had been better or we had a better time frame. I spent days going over and over in my mind what I could have done to save this venture. I felt like a complete failure. I couldn't let it go. I beat myself up worse than anyone else could have ever have beaten me up. Plain positive thinking was not helping me pull out of this emotional mess I was caught up in—I felt utter hopelessness. This feeling lasted several weeks and my life was pure hell.

Finally I'd had enough. I left my office, went home, shut off the phones, and didn't answer the door. I put on my PJs and bathrobe and allowed myself to just feel sorry for myself. I allowed myself to cry and feel the pain that I'd been trying to hide from everyone else. I gave myself permission to eat anything I wanted and as much as I wanted for that afternoon—I just let myself go. I let the rest of the world take care of itself for a few hours while I just wallowed in my own feelings.

While I was throwing myself this pity party, I had a bigger picture in mind. I didn't want to get caught up in feeling sorry for myself to the point that I gave up on myself, so I designed a safety net. At 6 p.m., no matter how I felt, I was to get dressed and get out of the house. I gave myself some options for breaking this mood: go shopping, eat out with friends, or go to the movies. I built a time limit into my emotional foxhole. I allowed myself to own and experience my feelings but I put a time limit on how long I would focus on them. And it worked—the next day I felt so much better! The fact that I failed at something was still a reality, but emotionally I was over it. I had allowed myself to grieve the loss, and now I could move on.

I've been speaking to audiences since 1980 about strategies for using human potential. I used to teach that when you were having a bad day or buckling under a negative problem, use positive affirmations, listen to motivational tapes, and do a pattern interrupt to break the negative flow. These strategies clearly still work because if you are merely temporarily off balance, repeating affirmations and listening to tapes will change your focus. Whatever you focus on always expands. Changing your focus from what is wrong in your life to that which is good will leave you in a more positive, resourceful state of mind.

I am now taking the concept of nurturing and loving yourself during difficult times to a deeper level. There are times when you must give yourself permission to create an emotional foxhole. There is no question that we all have physical sick days and we also have emotional sick days. Days when we are filled with fears and lack faith in ourselves or the future because we are overwhelmed with life and dealing with our responsibilities. What I have come to discover over the past few years, from my own personal experience and the experience of others, is that if you don't confront and deal with your emotions you may deny yourself one of the most important aspects of being alive—*your true feelings*. In doing this you suppress your frustrations to the point that you "go off the deep end" over something insignificant and vent your wrath on innocent bystanders. You need to find an outlet that allows you to get out of your negative state of mind and still honor your feelings. Some good outlets are fishing, bubble baths, walking, meditation, gardening or almost any hobby. In an effort to use your energy resources to your greatest advantage, take the time to deal with your feelings right away. Most often you won't have the time or the environment to be able to have a day at home. I don't either so I've developed some other ways to get over personal setbacks or hurts.

One strategy that I find really works for me is writing out how you feel about what's happening at the moment you feel upset. Just start writing away in your journal about how you feel. Express your true thoughts about how hurt, frustrated, scared, angry, or overwhelmed you feel. If someone else has taken advantage of you, write them a letter telling them how you feel about what they did, exactly what you think of them, and what you would like them to do to stop hurting you. Of course—never, never send the letters! The purpose of this exercise is to honor how you are feeling and vent the pent-up feelings out of your body and mind. You no longer have to go through the day having imaginary conversations with others about what you would like to say to them. Do it on paper. The magic of this exercise is that you will feel absolutely relieved to have gotten it out of your system.

After you've allowed yourself to own your negative feelings and to grieve your losses, it's time to move on with more empowering strategies that will allow you to regain your control. When we get depressed or have anxiety attacks, it's because we feel we've lost control. We have given up our responsibility of what information we are putting into our computer, our brain.

Your thinking process creates your emotions; your emotions control your behavior. When you accept the responsibility for your own thoughts, you can control your feelings. It's good to give yourself time to experience your emotions and own them. After a short time, however, you need to do a pattern interrupt on yourself, because what you focus on expands. Change your focus—go do something that is fun or rewarding to you. Separate yourself from the situation. Making a big mistake doesn't make you a failure.

When you make a mistake or have a failure, treat it as the exception. Say to yourself, "This isn't like me; next time I will succeed." I used to love to watch the old Bloopers TV show; it reminds me how to treat my mistakes—cut them out and do retakes! There's no need for guilt or punishment if you learn from the experience and try again. Refocus your life energy and attitude on the positive and be supportive of yourself. Treat yourself as you would your best friend. Give yourself permission to experience life and not hide from it.

FOUR POSITIVE WAYS TO DEAL WITH A BAD DAY

Sometimes life becomes so demanding with pressures from work, family, home, and social life that we need the adult equivalent of Linus's blanket from the Peanuts cartoon. Here are some tips for when you feel overwhelmed:

1. Try to get to a place you can be alone. Imagine yourself in your favorite place or a quiet, peaceful location such as in a forest, on the top of a mountain or by the waterfront—a mental Shangri-la. Not only is this an excellent pattern interrupt but this type of imagery allows you to focus on something beautiful and emotionally rewarding. The University of Delaware has done studies proving that imagining a quiet natural scene in your mind will significantly reduce your stress.

2. Another way to gain control over your emotions is to simply breath deeply several times. When your heart is beating too fast because of your anxious feelings, controlled breathing slows your heart and allows you to feel in control again. Breathing is also an effective form of muscle relaxation.

3. Much of the stress we feel is a result of our own thoughts, so if we can think ourselves into a stressful state, we can think ourselves into relaxation. Thoughts that are relaxed make our muscles relax. Controlling your self-talk will instruct your mind to feel better and ease away the pressures of the demanding world. Some Declarations that are helpful are:

I am now calm and cool under all circumstances.
I am in control of my life.
I now can let go and relax.
I am in control of all my thoughts and actions.
I am very effective and efficient in stressful situations.
I love and honor myself.
I have a positive attitude that I can handle myself in all situations.

4. Give yourself permission to appreciate yourself by having some positive personal rewards, such as a massage; pampering yourself with a salon treatments, manicure, facial; a good meal (with dessert); a night out on the town; a hot bubble bath and a glass of champagne; phoning someone you love to give you a lift; a cleaning service to clean your home. Anything that empowers you to feel like you are special! Always keep in mind that bad days don't last. This too shall pass. Empower yourself not to let your state of mind control you—you always control your emotions with your thoughts.

EMPOWERING QUESTIONS TO ASK YOURSELF WHEN FACED WITH AN EMOTIONALLY-ILL DAY

What can I do today to get away from the world and just take care of myself?

What can I do to have a good day today in spite of reality?

What resources can I use today to get back to my normal positive-thinking self?

What friends will be a support system, with whom I can share my problems?

What self-talk can I start to use now to change my state of mind?

In what areas of my life have I allowed myself to be a victim? What do I want to do differently in the future?

In what things in my life do I demand that I be perfect?

In what areas of my life am I out of balance?

In what activities am I trying to be all things to all people?

Where in my life am I stuffing my feelings and not venting frustrations?

How can I not take myself so seriously?

In one year from today, what will be funny about this situation or my behavior?

CHAPTER
_15_
ENJOY LIFE!
THIS IS NOT A DRESS REHEARSAL

Life is a journey, not a destination. How much we enjoy this journey depends on how we use our life energy. One of the most important skills we need to have in today's accelerated life style is a sense of humor. We need to stop taking ourselves so seriously. It's very easy to get caught up in reacting to life and not see how serious you have become. I personally didn't realize how seriously I took myself until this incident opened my eyes.

I was out one day taking care of several small errands and had my twelve-pound toy poodle, Murphy, with me in the car. I had just picked up some printing for the office and laid it on the front seat. I had to get out of the car to run into the post office for just thirty seconds to mail a letter, and I put Murphy in the back seat so he wouldn't jump all over the fresh printing. I backed away from my car toward the post office door saying, "Now stay. Be good. I'll be right back. Don't move!" I literally bumped into a guy who was holding the post office door open for me and who gave me this advice: "Lady, I usually just put my car in park!"

Taking yourself too seriously cuts down on your opportunities to enjoy life. We should think of life as an adventure and enjoy the moments. Look for the lighter side of every situation and don't hesitate to laugh to yourself if it's warranted. Every time you laugh you increase your body's level of endorphins. Those are the "feel good" hormones which imitate morphine in the body. Research also suggests that laughter can, in fact, help improve resistance to pain and disease.

Consider the example of Norman Cousins who wrote the book *Anatomy of an Illness*, describing his remarkable recovery from terminal illness by the use of humor and laughter. He made a firm decision that he was going to live, so he collected all the humorous material he could find: "Candid Camera" episodes, Marx Brothers films, books, and comedic movies. He then proceeded to literally laugh himself back into health; he did everything he could to make himself laugh so his body would heal. Cousins said the point was that the laughter didn't simply lead to health; it *was* health. It's the best mental health course you can take. Research states that humor ignites the will to live, which when missing, makes the recovery process very difficult.

When I decided to become a professional speaker I realized that I was never going to be perfect. Since I had chosen this profession, I'd better allow myself to laugh at my own mistakes and enjoy it! As a matter of fact, I make every mistake there is. From time to time, I forget what I'm talking about if I get distracted. I mispronounce words, and occasionally I find myself inventing words on stage. And once I even fell off a stage! I've been amazed and surprised at how my humanness has endeared me to most of my audience. (Though not everyone; I'm convinced that God could stand in front of some people and they would find something wrong!)

On my first international speaking tour, I was the lead speaker for a huge convention. The meeting planner pulled me aside before I went on to say that the audience was very subdued and he wanted to do something that would excite them before I began. His idea was to give me a drum roll as I ran out on stage, and this would help to wake them up. Well, I'm a sport so I agreed; as the drum roll started I ran out on the stage. Halfway across I tripped, fell, and rolled right off the stage—you can bet they were awake now! And of course, I felt like an absolute fool! I had to think fast, so I jumped up and made a joke. I said, "Don't be alarmed, that was my Chevy Chase imitation." They all just stared at me—it's not my fault they didn't know who Chevy Chase is!

But I laughed at myself, relaxed and started my speech. The advantage of my lighthearted response was that I was able to acknowledge my mistake and joke about my predicament. When I resorted to a self-deprecating routine and made fun of the situation, I was conveying grace under pressure with confidence and credibility. It's always important to remember that, to live a reasonably happy life and be able to respond appropriately to difficulties and adversities, you need the ability to laugh. Using humor can do more than just save you from embarrassing situations. It can make a remarkable difference in your self-esteem, as well as in how you set and approach goals. You will handle relationships better and keep life in perspective.

Another time I overcame an unfortunate circumstance in my life was at a major hotel in Florida. I had just enjoyed room service while preparing for my speech on Professionalism and Self-image, scheduled for the next day in the same hotel. After a steaming bath, I put on my favorite white night shirt which I noticed had shrunk considerably in the last wash. Planning to retire for the evening, I slid the tray into the hallway while attempting to hold the door open with my foot. Before I knew what had happened, the door clicked shut behind me, leaving me—to my horror—stranded in the hallway clothed only in that shrunken T-shirt!

With no rescue in sight, I did the unthinkable and traversed the very public lobby to retrieve a key, all the while stretching my night shirt to its limits. As I was attempting to patiently point out why I had no identification to the clerk, the man in line behind me queried, "Aren't you the speaker tomorrow morning on image and professionalism?" At the same moment, I caught a glimpse of myself in a nearby mirror reflecting my mascara-streaked face, standing-on-end hair and *thin* T-shirt. Mustering my best disposition, I smiled and replied, "Yes, this is the Before Look, tomorrow you will see the After Look!"

Not only did I save face at a very embarassing moment, I capitalized on the situation the next day when I started my speech. I told the story and had the entire room in stitches within minutes. This was a perfect start for my day! Don't worry if you feel your sense of humor has been dampened in the past. You can learn to use humor with a little practice, patience, and a willingness to let the lighter side of life shine through.

Learn to Lighten Up

Your emotions are created by your thoughts. To stop taking yourself so seriously, it's important to create an internal environment that supports you. To deal with the stress of life, it's important to be able to laugh at yourself. Let's face it, there will be a lot of things you cannot change and the better your sense of humor, the better you're going to feel about you and your life. Humor keeps us sane and gives us a sense of balance. Remember when you were a child; children love the absurdity of life. They do things for the sheer joy of it—they don't care about what others think. They do things simply to have fun.

Life is too short to not have some fun and give ourselves the ability to play again. Begin the process of lightening up with these homework assignments:

Comic Relief

1. Even if you don't consider yourself a good joke teller, tell a joke everyday for the next 21 days. (It can be the same joke told to 21 different people.) Allow yourself to enjoy telling jokes to make others laugh. The more you do it the better you will become.

2. At least once a month, go with friends to the local comedy club or an entertaining play. One of the reasons why an entertaining night of comedy leaves you feeling so good is that it helps you forget all your troubles for a short time and just laugh. (Not to mention all the great jokes you'll pick up and be able to tell later!) The value of laughter is that it enables you to gain a new perspective on your problems. Exposing yourself to humor can often help you realize others have the same problems and you're not

the only one.

3. Watch funny television shows, go to funny movies. Life is serious enough without compounding it by watching drama, soaps, and the news.
4. When you read your local newspaper, turn to the funnies first. The strategy allows you not to take the negative news so seriously.
5. Associate yourself with people who are funny, optimistic, and enjoy life.
6. Pretend you're a writer for the *Tonight Show*, and look around you for humor everywhere. It's there if you will look for it.

I used this last homework assignment to look for humor while I was on a long trip away from home. One day, on a flight from California to Phoenix, Arizona, the captain came on the speaker system to point out that we were over northern Arizona. He explained that a huge meteor fell from the sky thousands of years ago and left an enormous crater in the ground when it hit the earth. A young teenager was seated next to me and we both looked out the airplane window at the same time. He then sat back in his seat, turned to me and said, "You know, if that meteor had fallen a few feet to the right, it would have hit the highway!"

Learn To Say Four Phrases At The Appropriate Time To Help You Lighten Up And Stop Putting Pressure On Yourself:

1. *I don't know.*

Many times we won't say "I don't know" because we're afraid others will think we're incompetent. In reality, you're just human and can't possibly know everything. It's okay to not know everything—no one does. And you can always say, "I can find out and let you know later."

2. *I need help.*

Everyone needs help from time to time. Many of you have your superman and superwoman capes on today; no one can be all things to all people. Unfortunately you're going to burn out without a support system. Saying "I need help" must be done at the appropriate time.

As an example: if your boss has given you a new project and you're already up to your eyeballs in past-due work, you may want to say to your boss, "I can get this project done, but I'm going to need some help if you also want my required work done on schedule."

There is one place I recommend that you rephrase "I need help" and that is at home. When you say I need help with the housework or yard work, you're implying that it's all your job. Since we teach people how to treat us, be careful not to take on more responsibility than necessary. How about saying, "I need you to share responsibility for the housework or yard work."

3. *I was wrong.*

When you're wrong, admit it. Because if you don't someone else will be pointing their fingers at you saying it for you. I recommend that you apologize only once, then take your energy and go right into problem solving. Ask "What can we do to fix this situation?"

4. *Learn to say "no" at the appropriate time.*

How many times have you overbooked yourself? Gotten involved with a project that you didn't have time for and didn't want to do in the first place? A tip I learned from a time management class: I went through my calendar and wrote "BOOKED" on my weekends and free time. Now when people ask me to do things and I'm not sure if I really have time or want to get involved, I tell them "I have to check my calendar, I might be booked, I'll get back to you." This strategy allows you to choose what activities you really want to become involved with instead of being a reactor and over-booking yourself.

It's hard saying no to people because we want them to

like us. We end up giving too much of ourselves because we don't want to disappoint anyone. The position I take now is that I would rather they be disappointed and that I suffer the sixty seconds it takes to decline with kindness. It's better for me to be honest with myself than suffer by ending up doing things I don't have time to do.

Look at the Big Picture

I must admit that developing a great sense of humor took some nurturing. One of the tricks that has empowered me to deal with life is to observe other people and to use their strategies whenever possible. About the same time I started my speaking business, I met a great woman, Mrs. Vance, who was in her late seventies. She had been a successful business woman, had raised three children, had traveled around the world, and had been married to the same man for over fifty years.

In my opinion, she was a major success. I took her out to dinner one evening and asked her to please share with me the most important wisdom she had learned in her life. She looked me in the eye and said, "Don't take yourself so seriously and don't ever sweat the small stuff!" She went on to say that at her age she can honestly say that almost *everything is small stuff!* She went on to say, "Not living in the present and truly enjoying your life is the biggest mistake you can make. When I was younger I missed out on a lot of good adventures because I tried to live up to what other people said being a good woman was supposed to be. I was so busy taking care of other people's needs and desires that I didn't take care of my own. I regret, when I look back on my life, the time I wasted being upset over the silliest things. Now that I'm in my seventies, if I could change my history, I would care less about what other people had to say about how I lived my life. I wish I had enjoyed more sunsets with my family and played more with my kids and husband, instead of keeping a perfect house and trying to impress others."

One day I called Mrs. Vance and asked her if I could stop by and say "Hello" since I was in her neighborhood.

After she served tea, I noticed several get-well cards on her fireplace mantle. I was concerned, so I asked her how long she had been ill. She laughed and replied, "Oh, I haven't been sick for years. I'll let you in on a secret; I like to have fun and play a joke on some of the uptight, perfectionist people who expect me and my home to look like an ad from *House and Garden* magazine. I keep these get-well cards out for when I have unexpected company and the house is a wreck!" We both laughed. (By the way I'll be saving any get well cards I may receive in the future to use for the same purpose!)

-16-
HOW TO PROJECT CONFIDENCE AND PROMOTE YOURSELF

Simply working hard doesn't put you ahead anymore. To be successful in today's competitive world you must do more than have the right background, earn the right college degree, or know the right people. You must learn how to successfully promote yourself within your own profession, company, and community.

The purpose of this chapter is to expand your awareness and give you food for thought on how to be more visible, build connections, and position yourself to see new opportunities. It will also give you strategies that nearly all successful people use. Just as athletes look to master coaches, success cadets must study the methods of outstanding successful and visible people. You must invest in yourself and understand that self-marketing is a necessary ingredient in the demanding and changing world in which we now live.

Our educational system and society in general have not taught us the importance of promoting ourselves for visibility. We have been brainwashed by society that it is unacceptable to do anything but wait for others to notice our achievements and our talents. Most of us feel we must be shy about our accomplishments and our potential; we shy away from tooting our own horns because it seems like we are bragging. We fear others will think we are being pushy and unprofessional to promote ourselves and create visibility within our company or profession. The bottom line is that personal publicity is not only professional, it's essential for success and personal validation. Getting ahead in today's competitive world means getting noticed, and you need good exposure to do that. I have heard experts in marketing say that good exposure is more than half the battle and six times more important than performance. Think about this: if you don't let your boss, associates, and clients or customers know that you're a capable, creative person who deserves recognition and respect, *who will?*

For you to prosper in the difficult climate of company cutbacks and an unsteady economy, you must update your awareness of the fact that success is determined by how an individual feels about himself. Being shy and not creating positive visibility for yourself will only keep you in the shadows. The people who are being promoted today, getting raises and prospering in these trying times, believe in their self-worth and the value of their services. They aren't shy about letting the world know what talents they can offer. They can't afford to be—the competition is too stiff!

The world has changed. All you have to do is pick up this morning's newspaper and you will see attorneys and physicians now advertising their services; the same ones who formerly did not publicly promote themselves because it was not considered professional or in good taste. Those were the old days; today's society accepts those who actively seek recognition for their work in a professional manner. These self-promoters aren't shy about telling the world of their products or services because they've learned that the results of self-promotion helps them earn more money, gain more respect, and cultivate more opportunities.

It's very clear that today's society respects and admires individuals who go out and make a positive name for themselves in their fields of expertise. Often, the most well-known personalities will be sought after simply because they are well-known and respected for their abilities. It's human nature for people to want to deal with winners, and people who promote themselves in a tasteful professional manner are winners.

In the real world, visibility has become a basic survival tactic. It's important to realize that without the understanding and/or motivation to be seen and known you will stay average in your field and receive an average income return on your time invested.

A press representative for the American Broadcasting Company in New York said, "Personal publicity means bringing yourself to the attention of others. Personal publicity develops and sharpens your image, draws attention to your activities and achievements, and invites opportunities for advancement by making people aware of you."

I am a firm believer that you do not have to reinvent the wheel in self-marketing. You can do something called modeling, which means using the skill of awareness in paying attention to the strategies of other successful people in your field. Start to notice what their strategies are for creating good results in visibility. Simply mold and shape some of their strategies into your own career style and personality. Tom Peters talks about being a smart idea stealer in his book *Thriving on Chaos*. Be a strong observer of others and what strategies get the best results for the least amount of effort.

I would like to share with you some of the strategies I personally used when I was starting my business as a professional speaker in 1980. I had a lot going against me—no previous experience and very little capital, added to the fact that we were in a recession at the time. Yet I beat all the odds against me because I used all the resources I've shared with you in this book. I also succeeded because of my determination to build a good reputation and obtain as much free advertising as possible. I have watched and studied successful people, and I know if there is a will there is a way.

Many people have found out the hard way that just being great at what you do isn't good enough—other people must know about you and want your services. Looking back on my career, I can easily pinpoint specific turning points that helped me not only survive in my career but prosper tremendously.

My first venture into self-marketing was to simply write up a press release about my new company and have a photo taken professionally; it appeared in my hometown paper. It was inspiring for me to see the announcement in print and hear people tell me they saw it. I naively thought the phone would then start to ring off the hook and I would have tons of business! (These illusions die hard!) Six months later, an executive from Chesapeake & Potomac Telephone company called to find out what I could offer their regional tri-state sales meeting. As we talked, I asked her how she knew about me; she replied that on her first day of a new job as Training Director, she saw my press release and saved it for this meeting. I got the job, and that one presentation at a sales meeting helped launch my career from a local level to a national level. After that meeting, a representative from AT&T, who heard me speak, asked me to write and perform in three national training videos for all the phone center employees. That opportunity led me to work for corporations all over North America!

The lesson here is to never underestimate the power of self-promotion! Taking note of that positive and powerful experience with press releases, I created another strategy for gaining good press. I wrote to the press in every city I spoke and invited them to my presentations! I simply spelled out the benefits of sending a writer to cover my seminars so their paper could add value for their readers. I did not ask for advance publicity; I sent them tickets and gave them compelling reasons why they would benefit from covering my seminars. I admit that this was somewhat of an unusual approach at the time to not ask for advance publicity. Over a five-year period, I literally had over 100 newspapers and magazines cover my seminars and write stories about me, giving me positive national and international exposure. I took advantage of this great press by creating an impressive press kit and sent it to potential clients as a way to attract more speaking engagements. Plus, when I sent invitations to other newspapers and included copies of previous press stories, they were more likely to send a reporter which gave them and me another story. I never could have paid for that much free advertising and received such great results!

During this time when I was actively seeking print

exposure, I decided to expand to the broadcast media. I believe in being prepared, so I took a short course at a local college on how to do television commercials and be a spokesperson. I also took voice lessons to rid myself of a heavy southern accent. I wanted the confidence to look and sound good on TV and radio. Using a strategy similar to the one that I had used with the newspapers, I targeted the local television and radio talk shows. I first sent them a letter proposing subjects I could talk about which would be informative and benefit their viewers or listeners. Within a short time, my efforts were rewarded and I became a regular guest on three different local shows. This exposure not only gave me valuable experience, but it helped me become better known and tap into business in my own hometown.

One fateful day, I called the producer of our local cable station to try to arrange an interview on their new real estate show. The producer was familiar with who I was and my work since he had seen me on other shows and readily agreed to the interview. After that interview, he was so impressed that he asked me to co-host a new television talk show called *Lifestyles*. The show was taped once a week and would not interfere with my speaking engagements so I gladly agreed. I went from co-host to host within a year and happily hosted the show for over six years. I'll admit they didn't pay me very much, so it wasn't a financial windfall for the first two years. But the entire experience provided valuable training for my future. Everything you do in life leads you to the next step. Having the foresight to learn new skills gives you valuable experience you will need in the future to take advantage of potential opportunities. Plus, having that show looked very impressive on my credentials out of town!

Using the same strategy I had with newspapers and magazines, I then started sending letters to out-of-town television and radio stations, letting them know when I would be in their areas for possible talk show interviews. Again, it worked! I began appearing on talk shows; the appearances not only helped my exposure in my speaking business, they also sold the audio and video tapes I had written and produced.

One of the nicest turning points in my life came when I was touring Canada giving seminars. I had sent the information to the *Dini Petty Show,* the number-one daytime television talk show in all of Canada. The interview I obtained went great and the show got a very good response from their viewers. The response was so great from that show that they liked me *and remembered me;* a few years later the *Dini Petty Show* producers asked me to join with my own advice segment once a week. This international exposure led me to national shows like *Sally Jessy Raphael, Sonya Live* on CNN, and countless other well-known television and radio shows.

I can truthfully say that without my self-marketing efforts, I would not have been successful or even survived in my career. The exposure has presented more opportunities to me than I could have ever realized if I had simply waited for my talents and knowledge to be noticed or for someone else to discover me.

I can have the most expensive and beautiful brochure on my services ever made (and I do); it never brings me business. What promotes the most business is word of mouth; a client read about me in a newspaper or magazine article and called to find out more information; another saw me on television or heard a radio interview and wanted to hire me or buy my audio and video tapes; still another saw me speak at a function and told other people about me.

I will also admit that I made a clear decision that I would be willing to spend the time and effort to promote myself; I was always willing to look at the long-term benefits. I also had a lot of fun on the journey to encourage my efforts which have been rewarded with great results. Keep in mind life is a journey—not a destination. You can make the journey fun and exciting or you can make it hard and difficult. It's your choice.

The following are some effective strategies for you to develop the high visibility that will help your career and income take off. Please be creative in molding and shaping these strategies into your own personal style, your environment, and your profession. Not all of the suggestions may be suitable for your needs at this time, but they will open the doors for creative thoughts on what strategies and resources you can use that would bring about your desire right now.

Be Your Best At What You Do

The first thing one must have is a good product. You are your product. The greatest public relations campaign cannot make up for a lack of substance. You must be the best you can be. Debbie Fields, founder of Mrs. Fields' Cookies, said that her best public relations approach was a good cookie. When she was a twenty-year-old newlywed, she began baking these soft, chewy cookies which were very popular among family and friends. She decided to open a cookie store and sell them. On the first day, when no one had bought any cookies, she decided to do a little public relations. She filled a tray with her new product and, going outside, she gave them away. Her strategy worked—people followed her back into the store to buy them! Today she has over seven hundred retail stores and still uses the sample free cookies to promote her products.

Attitude Adjustment Time

Your performance will depend on your attitude. Zig Ziglar, the famous motivational speaker and author, said, "Your attitude, not your aptitude, will determine your altitude." Self-promotion takes the right mental attitude and a time commitment. As an observer of life, I have noticed that the people who really make it not only focus on acquiring skills, but also on spotlighting them. They tend to look at self-promotion as something you do every single day as part of your career-building plan; you do not build a great reputation in a short time; it is done over a period of time with consistency and creativity.

Plan to Win

Improving your business image takes careful planning and flawless execution. First determine what you want to accomplish and what image you want to project. State your goals in specific terms and give yourself a timetable to get started. Always remember that intermediate targets will help you reach your goals faster. One of the golden rules of goal-setting is to give yourself enough reasons compelling you to go for your goal. Without the motivation and burning desire you will not feel the need or invest your time, energy, or money to create the professional visibility to propel your career to new heights.

There are many ways to showcase your skills and boost your professional prestige. How creative are you willing to be to use your own unique talents, skills, and experience to make yourself more visible?

Personal Appearance

You know the old saying, never judge a book by its cover; in reality we judge all people we meet in about thirty-three seconds. We "guess-timate" their ages, what they do in life, and their economic life styles, and, most importantly, we decide "should I respect this these people?"

All this means that if your look becomes outdated, people may assume your ideas are outdated too, and that you're not worth listening to or taking seriously. If your look is too flashy or ostentatious, people may assume that you might be too brash and noisy to be an effective diplomatic representative. It may not be fair, but most people assume that your outward appearance is a mirror of the person you are.

Don't take chances; seek out the advice of experts to make sure you look the way you want to appear, from your hair to your shoes. Professional image consultants are worth the investment. Whatever money you invest in your personal appearance will come back to you in confidence, respect, and additional business.

One of the ways to take advantage of appearance is to dress to be included. Most people tend to respond to others who look and act like themselves. According to Rosebeth Moss Kanter, author of the book *Men and Women of the Corporation*: "There is evidence from organizational studies that leaders in a variety of situations are likely to show preference for socially similar associates and they tend to help them get ahead."

First Impressions

Since experts agree that you do create a solid impression of who you are in the first meeting, there is a powerful strategy to be sure you create a positive impression of yourself upon meeting a new person—it's called the thirty-second commercial. This strategy needs to be well thought out and delivered with care. First, think of all the things you can say about yourself that will imprint a polished and memorable impression that you could recite in about thirty seconds. This opportunity knocks after someone has asked you what you do for a living or where you work. The secret to making this strategy work is a response that paints a positive, professional, and interesting picture of you in the other person's mind. Your commercial tells the listener who you are and what you do in terms they can relate to.

A wonderful example of a creative and fun commercial is from Caroline McCartney, one of the top agents for a leading real estate company. When someone asks her what she does for a living or where she works she responds: "I am proud to be a residential real estate agent with GSH Realtors in the Norfolk, Virginia, office. We sell a house every hour of every day." On the end of her commercial she adds: "I am also proud of the fact that I was made a member of the million dollar club," or "I was the top sales person in my company," etc.

What makes that commercial so good is that it is unique, concise, and informative with no bragging or boasting. It simply leaves people with a positive impression that this agent is excited to be in real estate and is proud of her company. Everyone who has had the pleasure of meeting Caroline is always impressed with her positive energy for her career and her desire to be of service to people. It just so happens that the statement, "we sell a house every hour of every day" was at one time the company's logo. She just capitalized on a very catchy phrase as an approach to be memorable. And it works!

This commercial strategy needs to sound and feel natural so be sure you draft a few different ideas that match your personality; test them out to decide what commercial will empower your image to your best advantage. It's important to remember that the more light-hearted you are—the more you have fun with this strategy—the more effective it will be. People like to associate with people who have fun personalities and don't take themselves too seriously. Another important factor in making a powerful first impression is your outlook on life. Whatever attitude you project into the world will be reflected back to you. Always be a positive talker, looking for the good in whatever situation possible. Be *for* things instead of against things; instead of complaining about the pollution, concentrate on your own recycling efforts. When people ask you how you are, don't use the standard "Fine" or "Okay," impress them with "Things are great" or "Business is good!" The truth is, no one wants to hear negative information and you will never build a good image if you are negative and focusing on what is wrong with life. It goes without saying that when you introduce yourself with self-confidence and connect with the other person with a firm handshake, people notice; more importantly, they are more likely to take you seriously. Whenever you shake hands, your left hand should be reaching into your left pocket for that most effective promotional tool, your business card. Visual reinforcement of the verbal name will make you more memorable. Direct eye contact, a ready smile, and a genuine willingness to listen—all these small touches help make someone feel special.

Be in Sales

All good sales people know that the true secret of success is making another person feel special and validated. Keep in mind that we are all salespeople. We are selling our time, knowledge, experience, energy, potential, creativity, and our personality. The better you are at selling your talents and abilities the more opportunities come to you. A leading university came out with a study a few years ago that said success in the business world was 94 percent "people skills" and 6 percent technical ability.

You have to sell your good qualities to others. A pleasant personality is one of the most important skills you can develop. Think about this: if the people you work with don't like you, they won't promote you or want you on their team. They certainly aren't going to tell you about positions opening up or support you in any way. You always receive from life what you reflect out. If you want support from others you must give it.

Charisma

Charisma is said to be the highest form of personal power. It is the magnetism and charm that attracts people to you. You do not have to be born with charisma; you can learn and develop it. The trick of finding out how to use your own natural charisma is to think about the areas in your life that you are very excited about, and simply transfer those feelings of excitement to your current career. Now, if you don't feel very enthusiastic about your current position, you need to think back to the beginning of your career and remember all the excitement and dreams you had—recommit your energy to getting back to that state of mind.

I call this "choosing what you have already chosen." To get excited and feel happy with your work you need to count your blessings for what is good about your work daily. You get what you focus on and if you spend your time thinking about what you don't like about your work, then on an unconscious level you are programming yourself to fail. Being enthusiastic and positive about your work gives you creativity and a desire to be outstanding.

Homework assignment: make a list of all the reasons you enjoy your work. List why you're grateful for your current position. Make a victory list of all your accomplishments. When you're feeling down, review your list to regain your energy for your work again. Success in life for anything you do is a planned result.

Do a Self-Inventory

The Chairman of General Electric Company, John Welch, said, "A strategy is trying to understand where you sit in today's world, not where you wish you were or where you hoped you would be, but where you are. It's trying to understand where you want to be five years out. It's assessing the realistic chances of getting from here to there."

Ask yourself these empowering self-inventory questions: What strategies are you currently using to market yourself in your profession or career? What are your strengths? What can you do to capitalize on them? What are your weaknesses? Who or what could help you overcome your marketing weaknesses?

THINGS TO DO TO GET A PROMOTION OR RAISE

1. *Be in the top 20 percent of your field or profession.* One of the obvious reasons to be in the top of your profession is that you will always have the first opportunities for advancement. From a security point of view, being at the top gives you leverage, because no matter what happens to your company, you will always be in demand. Also, company owners never get rid of their very best people during cutbacks.

2. *Take the initiative.* Be self-motivated to get things done. Suggest ways to save money or time.

3. *Be well informed.* Keep up with trade magazines or other sources of information for your profession. Stay current in your career with the latest developments and breakthroughs. Become a trend spotter!

4. *Be the source of new business.* Find ways to increase your companies clients, and customers.

5. *Be willing to work overtime.* Be seen as a person who will do whatever it takes to get the job done.

6. *Volunteer for assignments.* This strategy can create a cross-training environment where you learn more than just the job you now have. You and your company both benefit from this type of involvement. You are more versatile, more valuable, and more marketable!

7. *Be innovative.* Find ways to save your company money or time. Remember—a dollar saved is a dollar earned! Creating profit for your company will make you very visible.

8. *Be a team player.* Team stands for Together Everyone Accomplishes More. Cooperation is a crucial skill. You may not like all the players, but you need them to win the game.

9. *Be reliable.* Do what you say you are going to do. Be on time with commitments. If you know you cannot be on time with your previous commitments, negotiate a new time.

10. *Be decisive about your decisions.* Gather all the information you can and make a decision; if it turns out to be the wrong one, cut your losses and select another direction.

11. *Be a master of detail.* Most people don't remember how fast you did the job, but how well you did it.

12. *Pad your employment file with favorable comments.* Take the initiative and write a weekly or monthly progress report to give to your boss. Keep copies on file for your performance evaluations.

13. *Look for positions in money-producing departments.* In an era of cutbacks and downsizing, it's wise to position yourself, if possible, in areas that support the company with incoming revenue.

14. *Take advantage of company-sponsored training programs or tuition reimbursement programs.*

Being a lifetime learner is one of the surest ways to get ahead in any company and ultimately in life.

15. *Be a leader.* There is a difference between managing and leading. You can manage only yourself; however, you can lead others by being a good example.

16. *Be honest.* Having integrity and high values counts more than ever today. Being trustworthy can increase your chances for upward mobility.

17. *Be a motivator.* Catch people doing things right! Offer to give training sessions or workshops in your expertise to others.

18. *Network.* Use your free time such as lunch, coffee breaks, and after work to expand your group of friends and cultivate new contacts. Build new alliances with others in different companies. Information is power.

19. *Be curious and open-minded.* When you are curious you learn; when you learn, you have valuable information to share.

20. *Be a visionary.* See the big picture: how can your talents, experience, and time help your company reach its goals?

21. *See yourself as a salesperson.* You have inside clients: your boss, and your co-workers; and you have outside clients. Be sure you are serving all your different clients' needs. Have a pleasant personality.

22. *Be the ambassador for your company.* Have positive things to say about your firm. Send any articles of business interest or promotions to your professional contacts with a personal note to keep your name and company's name in front of them.

23. *Ask for a raise or promotion.* If you really deserve it; remember, if you don't ask they will think you are happy where you are. A true secret of life is to ask for what you want.

24. *If you cannot get a raise, go for a new title.* Titles can be used as leverage should you decide to go look for a new job in another company.

25. *Be persistent.* Claude M. Bristol wrote *The Magic of Believing* and said: "It's the constant and determined effort that breaks down all resistance, sweeps away all obstacles."

PROGRESSIVE EXTERNAL STRATEGIES AND RESOURCES FOR GAINING VISIBILITY

Photos

A picture can say a thousand words and will leave a positive or negative impression. You need a current photograph of yourself. Invest in a recent attractive portrait taken in your best business attire. There is a very logical reason why photos help promote you: in general, people tend to be visual learners—they can remember you a lot easier if they can associate a face with your name. You never know when you will need a good picture of yourself because someone has written a story about you or you've announced your new promotion and the newspaper wants a picture of you to go along with the write-up. A word of caution: out-of-date photos, out-of-style makeup, clothes or hair will hurt your image. Have new pictures taken every two to three years. For sales people, having your picture on your cards or brochures make you more memorable to the people with whom you are dealing.

Press Releases

The old saying "out of sight is out of mind" is very true in today's fast-paced society. Another important strategy to help you become known and respected in your field is to send out press releases when you've done something noteworthy. For example, if you've been elected an officer of your professional association or just received a promotion that is noteworthy or become the new chairman for a charity committee. All these things are newsworthy and are reasons to send out press releases.

Please do not overlook getting free press from any of the newspapers in your community where you live and work. Send your press release to the newsletter of your professional trade and civic organizations. Don't forget your alumni journals. You'll be amazed at the number of publications you can contact who are hungry for information to fill space in their pages!

Publicity releases are not hard to write and can have very powerful results as I shared previously about my own career. The information you want to announce should be stated clearly and succinctly in the first paragraph. Your headline should be catchy and state your objective in five or six words. The release should coherently cover your main points, backed up with facts and opinions. Include a studio-quality black and white photo with your press release. A follow-up phone call is recommended to make sure the editors got the release and to see if they need any additional information.

Free Advertising Through The Broadcast Media

As producer and host of a cable talk show for over six years, I can tell you truthfully, from having been in that position, that producers are hungry for new people who are experts in their field. The television and radio media uses up resources and people almost faster than it can replace them.

You can benefit your career and your good reputation, as well as truly be of service to the viewers, by appearing on local television and radio programs. Getting booked on local broadcast is as simple as having something new to say and letting a producer know about it.

Your first focus should be on what areas you can become a media expert or resource. Your topics could be anything people want to know more about; anything that improves their lives and almost anything controversial is material for the talk shows. The important thing is to come up with answers to problems that the general public want to know.

Your next step is to track down all local television and radio talk shows and find out who the producers are and how to contact them. The "first time" approach that works best with producers is to first write them a cover letter telling them that you have a topic that you could talk about and why you are qualified to talk about it. Let the producers know why their viewers or listeners would benefit from this information. Be sure you tell them in your letter about any other interviews you've done and on what subjects. Enclose as much material as you can to establish yourself as an expert in your field, such as your calling card, company brochure, newsletters, copies of articles in trade papers or newspapers where you have been interviewed or quoted. Create and include a biography with your awards and education. One of the secrets of creating rapport with producers is to make their lives easy. Enclose a series of self-written questions about your subject with angles, hooks, and slants. If you are trying to appear on television, you will also need to enclose a recent good-quality photo.

It's important that you follow up by calling to introduce yourself to the producer within five days after they have received your material; reinforce in person your desire to be a source for any upcoming show. Your desire is to create a good rapport with the producers and for them to remember you and use you on their broadcasts. You must ask for the opportunity for an interview. Professional, friendly persistence is the key. Just because producers might not be interested at this time doesn't mean they won't be interested in a few months. You need to also be aware that media people can be very transient and they move around from station to station. The producer you deal with today may very well be at another station in a month, so keep in touch. Please do not underestimate the power of television and radio interviews. Media exposure can give you such an edge because it establishes you as an expert on the subject matter and gives you credibility, not to mention the fact that the exposure is worth thousands of dollars in free advertising for you and your company or product.

Preparing For The Interview

Once you've finally gotten your interview date, you need to prepare to be very good on the show. You must do your homework and get to know the territory before you do your first interview. First, know your subject inside and out. Find out the format of the show—will it be live or taped? Will you be alone or on a panel with other people? If it's on the radio, will the interview be in the studio or will they call you on the telephone? What is the scheduled time for the segment and how much time do you have? Will there be listeners' calls? Who is the audience? How old are they? Are they mostly men or women?

It is crucial that you take the time to have observed the interviewer's technique. Spending the time to familiarize yourself with the style of the show and the host will help you feel more comfortable and prepared. A word of caution: if you don't know all the answers to the above information, you may be caught off guard and not excel in your interview; you risk looking foolish or ill-prepared, which damages your credibility. You won't be asked back if you don't do a great job.

Once you have your time limit, you need to plan your message of what information you want to share with the audience. It's important to brainstorm what questions will be asked and then plan how to handle them. Make sure that your information is delivered in clear, concise, colorful comments. Without planning what you're going to say, you may ramble on and on, never getting to the point. This makes it more difficult for the interviewer to capture the essence of your message. One great strategy is to practice many times on videotape, even if it's a radio interview, so you can review any speech or physical habits that are not becoming or could be distracting to the audience.

One important note: make sure you videotape all television interviews and audio tape all radio interviews. You can not only critique them, but also use them as a demo, leverage to get you on other talk shows.

Interviews By The News Media

If you have the opportunity to be interviewed by the broadcast news, please remember that television and radio reporters live by the sound bite. Because of time limitations some live stores are short; some are just sixty seconds long. The reporters may interview you for ten minutes but only use one minute on the air. It may not seem like enough time to make your point. But if you plan ahead, prioritize your information, and practice, you can learn to say a lot in a little time slot. The rule of thumb is that short, punchy answers really work the best. The good news is all this hard work pays off; once you've established yourself as a good source, the producers will use you over and over again because you're a proven performer. You will be seen or heard by thousands of people and it can help you become more respected in your career.

How To Deal With Newspaper Reporters

Dealing with newspaper reporters is much like dealing with the broadcast media people. You first write to the editor of the section of the newspaper for which you want to be a source and introduce yourself. Enclose the same material as you would with the broadcast media, and follow up with a personal phone call. Again, your purpose for calling is to create rapport with the editor or writer and be considered a source of information about your field of expertise.

Thank-You Letters

It's important to keep in mind that all the media people with whom you come in contact are just like you and I. They want to be validated and feel appreciated for their time and efforts. Always follow up all interviews with a sincere thank-you letter, telling them the positive response you received from their interview and how you would like to have the opportunity to be of service again in the near future. You may also want to use this as an opportunity to suggest other topics for which you could be interviewed.

Creating Visibility by Sharing Information

This is the information age. The way to achieve power and influence is to share information that helps others. There are many ways to share information and become more visible in your career or profession. Volunteer to give a speech, conduct a workshop, or organize a panel on a topic that will empower people and give them new resources. Speaking to groups is one of the most powerful ways to make a strong impact and be remembered. Contact your local chamber of commerce, church groups, Kiwanis, and other civic clubs, schools, as well as your own company's personnel department. Speaking and teaching engagements provide unlimited opportunities to reach the public and your professional peers.

If you plan a workshop or presentation, always notify the local media about it. One way to do that is to create a handout and send it to the newspaper, television and radio talk shows with a cover letter or press release. All local media stations schedule noncommercial time for community concerns.

Another option for gaining positive visibility is writing articles on your expertise. Having your ideas published will give you a lot of credence and authority with the media, your peers, and clients. Many times articles may well prompt invitations to speak on the topic you wrote about or stir media attention where you are invited to discuss you views on air.

Starting Your Own Public Relations Campaign

Start today with a new attitude that you have the power to create positive public relations that will benefit your long-term intentions with your profession. Having this mental strategy doesn't mean you have a huge ego. It simply means you are willing to promote yourself as a basic survival tactic. Creating a positive image with your professional peers, your clients, and the general public takes time and effort, but the rewards will mean more respect, more clients, and more income. You also contribute to the good reputation of your industry and have more opportunities to create value for more people because they will know about your expertise and services.

You will find that, if you use these techniques, the benefits outweigh the effort and time investment. It's no secret that self-marketing is a science and an art. Start to experiment with what works for you, so you can achieve anything you are willing to focus on with your life energy. Keep in mind the quote from author James Allen, "You will become as small as your controlling desire, or as great as your dominant aspiration."

–17–
DESIGNING YOUR DESTINY

One cold rainy day in March 1985, I was in the Chicago airport waiting for a flight to Little Rock, Arkansas, when I spotted a tall, attractive man with graying blond hair who seemed to be at the center of everyone's attention. I boarded my flight and sat on an aisle seat. Just as I had settled, this same man took the seat across the aisle next to me. As the plane took off, a file folder fell off my lap; he picked it up and handed it back to me. The top of the file was labeled Arkansas Health Department. He asked about it, so I explained that I had been hired by the state of Arkansas to present a workshop on maintaining a positive attitude and goal-setting for their employees. I still had no idea who he was until he reached out his hand to shake mine and introduced himself as Bill Clinton, the Governor of Arkansas.

For the next two and half hours we talked nonstop about human potential and the power of setting clear definite goals. He told me of his belief that dreams and goals made the crucial difference between average and outstanding people. He told me about his dreams of what he could do to empower and help other people. He spoke of the powerful importance of having a dream and a clear plan of action if you wanted to be successful and make a difference in the world.

In the beginning of our conversation I had been skeptical; was he just being nice to me to get my vote? But, of course he knew that I was from Virginia and I couldn't vote for him, so I relaxed and just allowed myself to really listen. There we were, two people stuck on a plane together sharing some of our deepest thoughts and feelings about something we both felt very passionate about—reaching our goals and using our potential to empower other people.

As I listened to this man, little did I know I was talking to a future President of the United States of America, who sat next to me in coach class. I saw and experienced for the first time the love of country and commitment it must take for someone like him to be in political office. Up until that moment, I had, like many people, looked at many politicians as power-hungry and self-serving.

But on that flight, in a mere moment of time, my entire perception was changed. I learned from this man that there are some very sincere and caring people in the political system. People who really do believe that one person can make a difference if they stand up for what they really believe in and set high goals for themselves to make that difference. I also witnessed an individual who was so committed to his dreams that there was no way he would not reach them—even if it took his entire life. Whether or not you happen to like or agree with President Clinton, you have to admire him for his persistence in going for his beliefs and goals.

I believe that one of the most affirming ways to inspire yourself to set and achieve realistic goals is to look for role models. People who have clearly set goals for themselves find it has made a difference in their life and the people around them. By observing or getting to know these people, you can clearly see they had a strategy and plan that helped them achieve, earn, and obtain their dreams.

Normally I am not in favor of beauty contests; however, the 1990 winner of Miss America made me appreciate the power of setting a goal and sticking to it. Debbie Turner's dream was to become a veterinarian without any financial debt after finishing her degree. She entered the pageants as a means to win scholarships to finance her education. While a veterinary science student at the University of Missouri, Debbie entered the 1989 Miss Missouri Pageant after several failed attempts at the title in Arkansas, her home state. It took her over seven years and eleven pageants in two states to advance to the national finals.

Tracing her rise from being a scrawny, buck-toothed child to Miss America, her story was not about being a princess in a fairy land. Her parents divorced when she was six and she was told repeatedly that she would never become Miss America. But she refused to accept "no" for an answer; she believes that what you have on the inside is more important than what you have on the outside. After winning her crown she said, "If I had given up at the age of 16 when I entered and lost my first pageant, or if I would have given up after my 10th try, I would not be standing before you today, a brown-haired, brown-eyed, 5'7". southern minority Miss America."

It is role models like Debbie Turner and Bill Clinton who make you realize that you *can* create a future that is rewarding to you. Most people don't stick to their goals because they've not allowed themselves enough compelling reasons to stick with their dreams. They become discouraged and find the reasons why it's impossible to ever obtain their desires.

Charles Garfield, author of *Peak Performers*, has done extensive research on top performers in a variety of fields and found that the one characteristic all of them share is a sense of mission: "Whether focusing on family, developing talents, or getting to the top of a particular field, peak performers refine their capacity to clearly see what they want. Their mission provides the 'why' that inspires every 'how.'"

The downside of just setting goals is that our culture has a fast-food mentality; we expect instant gratification for short-term effort. Many times when you don't get instant gratification and see only short-term results, you give up on the goal. This short-term thinking prevents us from using our talents, experience, and life energy to create the long-term vision of achieving our dreams. Professional speaker Joe Griffith said, "A goal is nothing more than a dream with a time limit."

When I was in sales years ago, I remember setting goals for myself and, upon reaching them, I'd feel good for a day or so before finally feeling deflated. I had worked really hard only to reach the bittersweet realization that the next year's goals would have to top the goals I had just set. Over years of simply setting goals, it becomes harder and harder to get motivated and excited. Setting goals is not the problem here because having goals does serve a purpose.

The purpose is this—goals help us keep score by giving us something specific to go for with our life energy; they provide feedback to let us know how we are doing. The problem lies in the importance we attach to these goals. Goals are good for only one thing: what you become along the way because you chose them. If our goals are to be beneficial, they must be guided by something that inspires us with courage, creativity, and persistence. To sustain excitement and passion in your life you must have something to aim for that moves you, a dream you can chase. Robert Kriegel, in his book *If It Ain't Broke. . .BREAK IT!* said, "Dreams are goals with wings."

Your dreams can empower you more than anything else in life because they create a vision that motivates and inspires you. Dreams enable you to handle the setbacks and challenges of everyday living and can show you the way to turn a potentially negative situation to your benefit.

The right hemisphere of your brain deals with your emotions and imagination; it's where your dreams come from. Goals are created from the left hemisphere of your brain. Your goals are measurable, rational, and linear actions; they are the first step that must be taken to advance toward your dreams. Goals are tangible and supply the specific, short-term strategies. Your dreams may be intangible but they allow you to create the vision, emotion, and direction for what you want to manifest in your desired future. Dreams supply you with possibilities and potential and passion. Dreams engage your spirit and move you to new heights, allowing you to overcome self-imposed limitations from past programming.

Dreams give you the compelling reasons and motivation to stick to your tangible goals. They are the expression of optimism and desire; that energy is capable of guiding you through the uncharted territory of what you can accomplish, earn, acquire, or invent. The beginning of any adventure starts with a dream of the possibilities. Goals simply map out your options and strategies to help your reach your dreams. Businessman John Condry said, "Happiness, wealth, and success are by-products of goal-setting: they cannot be the goal themselves."

Mission Statement

Do you ever feel that life has not yet started for you? You're not clear about what you want to do with your life? Have you lost motivation for your goals? Do you catch yourself thinking, "Is this all there is?" And it seems that no matter how much you achieve, you feel something is still missing? If you have these type of feelings you need to be asking yourself: What has value in my life and what is my purpose?

This can be one of the most important questions you will ever ask yourself. Just going through life without a sense of purpose feels meaningless. After all, your purpose in life is the cornerstone of your motivation and your existence. Having a clear, well-defined purpose in life helps you get what you want. Purpose gives your life meaning, balance, and perspective. A clear life purpose helps you channel your energy constructively. Without a clear life purpose, your life can be spent in confusion and dissatisfaction.

Almost every successful company defines and publishes a mission statement. It's a statement about the mission of the company so the employees will understand the true purpose of company goals. To hit your target in life you have to be focused because what you focus on always expands. With so many options in the world, if we're not focused on what we want, we become scattered and continually shift our attention. When you have a purpose, you are in tune with the essence of whom you really are and what is important to you. That knowledge and energy will drive you toward your dreams and goals.

To be able to discover your purpose you need to first become clear about your values. You have to literally sit down and write out what has the most meaning to you—a personal mission statement. This statement allows you to capture the essence of your life and crystalize a direction. Defining your purpose provides you with a general connection to the world and allows you to see yourself in the big picture of life.

Your personal mission statement will change at different times in your life. If you're in school, your mission statement will look very different than if you are the parent of a newborn child or have a number of offspring to care for. Your retirement years will have a different type of mission statement than when you are just starting a new company. You should change or at least evaluate your mission statement on an annual basis by reviewing the changes you've made in your life and the circumstances impacting you.

Allow me to share with you my mission statement: I intend to live my life with perfect health, love, happiness, passion, creativity, flexibility, and to give love to myself and others. Now let me explain my formula. When I think about my life, one of my purposes is to share with others information that empowers them. I believe that one person *can* make a difference, and that one of our responsibilities is to be of service to mankind in some way. However, it is our first responsibility to take charge of our own lives and make sure that we love ourselves. That is why I also included "to give love to myself and others." You see, if I don't love myself, no one else can because I won't do the things necessary to create love.

To arrive at my statement, I simply listed my values, what has the most meaning for me. When I first started listing my values, I listed success as my most important value and love second. After studying my list I realized that success was a subjective thing, and the most important value in my life was my health. Perfect health is, to me, the truest wealth on earth. Without vitality and energy I could not accomplish my desires. The next value I added to my list was love and joy. Society has led us to believe that success, money, and titles are the most important goals. In reality those things are external influences. What is really important is how you feel on the inside. My list of values continued: passion, because I see myself as a very enthusiastic person; creativity, for I am driven to create and to experience many things; flexibility, as I have learned that flexibility is power—with the right attitude I can bend and grow when necessary. Other values on my list were spirituality, honesty, integrity, fun and adventure, excellence, intelligence, contributing, achievement, sharing, and harmony.

I suggest you record in your journal what is important to you. After you have become clear about what your values are, then write a one- or two-sentence mission statement. Being so concise lets you memorize it and reinforce it as a Declaration. Once you have a clear picture of what you want in life, your conscious and subconscious minds can work together to achieve it.

Write out your mission statement and put it in places where you will see it several times a day: your bathroom mirror, the refrigerator, your desk at work, maybe on the dashboard of your car. It's vital that you use the skill of awareness to be in touch with what is really important to you. If you don't reevaluate what has meaning, you'll end up spending your life chasing dreams that no longer have any meaning for you. The clearer you are about what you want in life and the resources you need, the higher your probability of achieving success, wealth, and happiness. It is simply the efficient use of your life energy. The more you focus your energy, the more powerful its impact. When you draw from your strengths, nothing can stop you.

Your life purpose provides you with inspiration. It's your reason for existing. Life purpose also carries you through those tough times when everything seems to be going wrong. Daily living has a lot of trials and tribulations that can get you down if you are not in tune with what your life is about. Your mission statement can give you power. Knowing what is important to you and what you really value in life strengthens your resistance to distractions of the outside world.

Code of Behavior

After you've written out your values you have to ask

yourself if you are living your life with integrity toward these values. One way to assure that you're living with your values in mind is to create what I call a Code of Behavior. List ten to twenty behaviors you can do daily that would improve you and allow your life to have more focus. This strategy allows you to become the person you really want to be. For example I wrote, I will be light-hearted, fun, flexible, positive, enthusiastic, resourceful, elegant, grateful, excited, curious, productive, forgiving, and conscious. It's important that you put your Code of Behavior next to your Mission Statement because you have to remind yourself to deliberately act in a manner that reinforces your life purpose.

Every Person Has the Power of Choice

Oliver Wendell Holmes said, "The greatest thing in this world is not so much where we are, but in what direction we are moving." Remember that you have the responsibility of choosing your own destination in life and every time you make a choice, you set in motion the power of the mind. Consider each of your thoughts to be like a seed planted in your future. There are no limits in life except the limits you set for yourself. You must be aware of negative choices because they use the same mental principles as your positive choices. And you will have to accept the fact that you are 100 percent responsible for what you choose for yourself because it will become your experience.

Question Your Past Programming

While a student in high school, I had a teacher named Mrs. Johnson, who gave a demonstration in class which left a major impression on me. It was a very simple experiment: she put some fleas in a glass jar and we observed how the fleas could jump right out of the jar very easily. Then she covered the jar, so the fleas were jumping up and hitting their heads on the top. In just a few minutes the fleas stopped jumping as high; in fact, they started jumping lower and lower. After about thirty minutes, Mrs. Johnson took the top off the jar and the fleas never jumped out. She was illustrating the analogy that we were like those fleas.

Society will condition you to not jump as high as you have the potential to go. You can be conditioned according to age, color, education, and stereotypes of your abilities. Life trains us to limit ourselves so we don't go for our dreams even when we have the talent, desire and potential. It's a great tragedy for people not to use the great potential within them.

Circuses train baby elephants by chaining them to a strong post. The baby elephant pulls, and tugs, becoming very frustrated, but he soon learns that he cannot get away. When the elephant becomes full grown and incredibly powerful, the handlers can still chain that elephant to a small post. Clearly, with the massive power of an elephant, it could easily pull up that post and go wherever it wanted to go. Yet the elephant has been conditioned that it cannot get away from the post and doesn't even try anymore.

Unfortunately, we humans also stop questioning at a young age where we excel and what we can achieve in life. Our past programming has, for the most part, not given us the encouragement to use all our talents and potential. There are no limitations in life other than the ones we put on ourselves. Most people do not succeed in life because they do not set goals that support themselves, making them realize their own power.

Don't Let Past Failures Hold You Back

It's important that you know that goal-setting takes courage. You must already know that living with integrity sometimes takes courage. So does standing up for your values. If you will look back on your life you will see hundreds of times when you've used courage to deal with reality. It's only realistic to understand that there will be obstacles—no one achieves a dream or goal without a few problems, hassles, and setbacks from time to time. But there is a fine line sometimes between being realistic and pessimistic.

Movie star and director Kevin Costner said, "I'm a big fan of dreams, and unfortunately, dreams are our first casualty in life—people seem to give them up, quicker than anything, for reality." Without a clear goal or dream you will not be ready to take risks or follow through with the necessary strategies to be successful. Failing at something in the past doesn't mean you will fail in the future. You now have more resources than you did before. If you fail and learn from the mistake you are a winner. You are only a failure if you make the same mistake over and over and do not review and change your strategy.

Flexibility Is Power

Pamela Pearce, one of the co-authors of *Reach Your Career Dreams,* said, "If failures could only learn to imitate the simplest laws of nature. Water, for example, takes the path of least resistance on its journey to the sea. When it comes to a rock, it simply flows around it. Failures don't do that. If they have a specific destination at all and run into an obstacle—a rock—they do not flow. They create a relationship with the rock. They then seek out other failures and complain about their rocks together. They tell each other they are winners for hanging in there."

Making adjustments and changing your strategies are important ways to stay on target. Sometimes it's important to know when to cut your losses and set another goal. However, never abandon goals just because they're tough or you've had a setback. Abandon goals or dreams only if they have lost meaning for you.

If, for some reason, you don't obtain one of your goals, don't judge yourself as if you were a failure. Goals, like everything else in life, must be flexible. Being flexible on how and when you reach your dreams gives you more power. Just because you didn't reach your goal this time, doesn't mean you can't reach the goals you want in the future.

Goal-Setting and Achievement is an Art and a Science

You are a goal-setter whether you realize it or not. What you accomplish is life is determined by the goals you clearly define and set for yourself. Setting definitive goals takes the tension and anxiety out of living. Setting goals is one of the proven ways to bring health, wealth, and happiness into your life. Goal achievement works because it is governed by specific mental laws. That to which you give your attention and that you believe is going to become your reality. This is the mental law of cause and effect—your thoughts materialize your future. The goals you set become the orders to your subconscious mind; your subconscious mind believes what you tell it and carries out your orders.

Goals Supply You With A Vision

President and CEO of Estee Lauder, Leonard Lauder, said, "Fantasizing, projecting yourself into a successful situation, is the most powerful means there is of achieving personal goals. That's what an athlete does when he comes onto the field to kick a field goal with three seconds on the clock, 80,000 people in the stands, and thirty million watching on TV. The athlete, like the businessman, automatically makes thousands of tiny adjustments necessary to achieve the mental picture he's forming of the successful situation: a winning field goal."

One way to start to see what you want is to relax and visualize yourself in the future. Simply giving yourself the opportunity to create pictures and feelings of achieving your goals will give you insights on easier ways to reach them. As an added bonus, every time you visualize yourself in your desired goal, you increase your confidence that you can reach your dreams!

Goals Makes Us Do More

As a boy, John Goddard dared to visit the magic kingdom of "What If." When he was fifteen years old, he made a list of all the things he wanted to do in life. That list contained 127 goals he hoped to achieve. It included such things as explore the Nile, climb Mt. Everest, study primitive tribes in the Sudan, run a five-minute mile, read the Bible from cover to cover, drive in a submarine, play "Claire de Lune" on the piano, write a book, read the entire *Encyclopedia Britannica*, and circumnavigate the globe.

Now middle-aged, he has become one of the most famous explorers alive today. He has reached 105 of his 127 goals and has done many other exciting things along the way. He is still looking forward to visiting all 141 countries in the world (so far he's visited only 113), exploring the entire Yangtze River in China, living to see the twenty-first century (he'll be seventy-five years old), visiting the moon, and enjoying many more exciting adventures.

Review *your* life and analyze how and why you've been successful in the areas that have the most meaning to you. If you are really truthful, you will see it was because you became clear about what you wanted, you focused your energy and took action. That is exactly what goals do for you. Goals give your brain a clear cut direction toward which to aim. Your brain is like a plane and it must be given a direction to reach your desired destination.

The Quickest Way to Get What You Want is Identify What You Want and Go For It

Yogi Berra said, "If you don't know where you are going, you might wind up someplace else."

There is an old story about advertising legend David Ogilvy, whose goal was to establish a great advertising agency within a dozen years. When he set this goal he was a small tobacco farmer in Pennsylvania. It is said that on his second day of business, he made a list of five companies he was determined to make his clients. The clients were: Campbell Soup, General Foods, Bristol-Meyers, Lever Brothers, and Shell Oil Company. Everyone told him he was crazy to think he could get these big accounts. He showed them—he was able to get all of them.

THE "HOW-TOS" IN SETTING GOALS
TO REACH YOUR DREAMS

Get in touch with your feelings or intuition about what you want.

Establish a purpose in life and write out your mission statement.

Identify the key resources to help you fulfill your purpose.
Set goals that are consistent with your overall purpose.

1. *The first step to reaching dreams is having them.* . .
Start asking yourself what you want in life. These desires must be realistic and obtainable. What is your intuition telling you about what you should be doing? Listening to your intuition is one of the most intelligent things you can ever do with your life energy. Your intuition always guides you in the direction that is perfect for you. It is that small voice that is not affected by egos, past failures, or other people's opinions—it is your inner guiding light. Throughout history, our teachers have taught us that all answers are within us. The way to access your answers is to listen to yourself. In your journal, keep notes on what your intuition tells you.

2. *Get excited about goal-setting.* . .
Talk to people and ask them how they achieved their goals. What was their strategy? How did they deal with setbacks? How did they form an action plan? How often did they review and alter their action plans? Remember, what you focus on expands. To motivate you to get into goal-setting, you must not try to reinvent the wheel; adapt the successful techniques of others into your own style, personality, and profession.

3. *Crystalize your thinking.* . .
Determine what specific goals you want to achieve. Your goals need to be specific, measurable, and realistic. To do this you'll have to avoid nebulous thinking, such as *I want to make a lot of money.* What does that really mean? For your subconscious mind to be able to serve you it must receive very specific directions.

4. *Develop a sincere desire for the things you want.* . .
Desire is the starting point for all achievement. It's the

greatest motivator of every human action. Frequently your mind is more motivated by pictures and imagination than it is with words and written exercises. The right side of your brain is where your creativity comes from and it thrives on pictures. Many times the right side of your brain takes precedence over the left side, which thrives on words. In the past, you may have just written words down to reach your goals. Add this new dimension to your process.

Draw, cut out pictures, or take photographs of what you want in life. For example, every three months I personally create something I call my Prosperity Board. I go to the drug store and buy a large green poster board. I divide the sheet into twelve different areas with a ruler. On the top of each area I write my main goal. I then collect as many pictures from magazines as I can find to represent as clearly as possible what I want to manifest in my life. Let's say you want a new car; get a picture of that car and put it on your Prosperity Board. If you decide you want that car in red but the picture you have is white, simply write red on the car. I also suggest that you put pictures up on your refrigerator and bathroom mirror, places that will remind your subconscious mind of your desires.

When I wanted to record my first audio tape program, I drew a picture of what I wanted it to look like and wrote "best seller" across the front of it as if it were an ad in a catalog. In my health goals, I put a picture of a healthy-looking salad and attractive people exercising.

Every thought you have uses electrical energy to imprint a new picture in your subconscious mind. The efforts of your subconscious mind are to match the pictures in your mind with reality. The more you deliberately plant pictures of what you want, the faster you will attract it into your life.

It's very important that you allow yourself to fantasize about what you want in your life—let your imagination run wild! To achieve what it is you want in life, you must *think about it*. There are no limits except those we put on ourselves. This is *your* life and you will be cheating yourself if you don't go for what you want! You must *feel* your success before you can manifest it in reality.

5. *Develop a plan for achieving your goal and a deadline for its attainment. . .*

The difference between a wish and a goal is that the goal is written down. Once you have a clear picture of what you want in life, your subconscious and conscious mind can work together to achieve it. When you can literally see what you want, you can prioritize and focus; this gives you concentration of power. Deliberate concentration is like a laser beam; it can cut through any obstacles in your path.

6. *Distinguish between goals and activities. . .*

A goal is the specific end result you want to manifest in your life. Activities are those things you do to achieve your goals. Use the skill of awareness; don't get stuck in the activities and forget what the goal is.

7. *Create deadlines for your goals. . .*

Without deadlines your brain doesn't have a clear picture of what you want created. Deadlines have a magical way of motivating us to produce results. They allow you to break down your long-term goals into short-term ones that feel attainable. For example, if you have a one-year goal, it's easy to put off getting started. You feel as if you're rich with time. However, that year passes quickly and suddenly you only have a short time to achieve your goal.

A better strategy: first write your one-year goals on paper; then write down all the activities you will have to do to reach your goal. Ask yourself these questions: What is the very first activity I must do to get started on this goal? Write that down; often simply getting started is the hardest part. Once you begin, you're on a roll!

Next question: What are the activities I must do in the first three months to achieve my goal? Then follow up with what activities in the next three months? By breaking down the goals into manageable, bite-size pieces, you'll feel more in control. This divide-and-conquer approach keeps your goals from becoming overwhelmingly complicated.

8. *Make your goals yours. . .*

Don't set a goal for yourself that your spouse (or anyone else for that matter) wants for you. Please revise your current goals to meet your needs, not someone else's desires for you. You will never be successful achieving goals that are not motivated by your desires. When you set goals, don't compare them with other people's goals—you'll always come up short. We usually compare our worst traits with someone else's best traits and we can never win that way.

I spoke to a convention a few years ago with television star Marlo Thomas. She told the story of how her famous father, Danny Thomas, had a long talk with her about following his footsteps into show business. He told her to put on blinders, like they do for race horses and run her own race. Never worry about what other people say or do—do your own thing!

9. *Write your goals as if they have already occurred. . .*

"I now earn _____, I now weigh _____ ," rather than "I want to earn _____ or I want to weigh_____." This allows your subconscious mind to see the end result.

10. *Develop confidence in yourself and your abilities. . .*

Stay "sold on yourself." Listen to motivational audio tapes daily in your car. Do your declarations daily and control your self-talk. Tackle every activity without giving any recognition to the possibility of defeat. Focus on your strengths instead of your weaknesses. Recognize and honor your powers instead of your problems. Develop a determination to follow through on your goals regardless of obstacles, circumstances, or criticism of what other people think or say.

11. *Make your goals realistic and congruent. . .*

I presented a Career Development seminar in Washington, D.C., a few years ago, after which a government employee came up to me complaining that goal-setting did not work. I asked him, "What is your goal?" He replied, "I want to be a millionaire." I asked him if he did anything that could help him earn the money to become a millionaire beyond his job. He said no, he couldn't think of anything else to do with his life, though he was still clear he wanted to be rich. The problem is that this goal was not congruent with what he did for a living and you never get something for nothing. You have to make your goal obtainable or you need to give up that goal. Don't set unrealistic goals for yourself if you know in your heart you're not willing to pay the price for achieving them. Setting yourself up for failure will only fuel frustration and cause you to lose confidence in yourself.

12. *Keep your goals to yourself. . .*
If you are excited and charged up about your dreams, you'll want to share this information. Don't—too often you'll hear how everyone else has failed while trying what you want to do. Their negative energy and opinions will sabotage your enthusiasm and faith in your abilities. Years ago I made the mistake of telling some people that I was going to be a successful international professional speaker—I had to pick them off the floor from laughing! Even worse, their negative attitude affected my belief in my abilities for several months. I learned from that experience to never share my dreams with anyone who might try to shoot them down. In our culture we are given the subtle message that "other" people are smarter than we are. If you share your dreams with people who are not part of your support system, they will undermine your confidence—keep your own council. Keep your dreams to yourself so you do not scatter your creative energy. Tell your dreams only to people who support you, are happy for you, and believe in your abilities.

13. *Review your goals monthly. . .*
The first day of the month is the perfect time to set up a ritual of goal-reviewing. This should be the time that you can be honest with yourself on what goals you are really committed to and how you can improve your strategies for achieving those goals. You must also be honest with

yourself on what goals are only paper dreams if you aren't really going to pay the price to achieve them. In the book *CareerTracking*, Jimmy Calano and Jeff Salzman recommend using the "Four R's test." Scrutinize your goals in terms of:

—Revising ("I still want to achieve this goal, but not quite in the way I had planned.")

—Removing ("I'm no longer interested in reaching this goal; I think I'll scratch it.")

—Rescheduling("I'll set a new, more realistic deadline.")

—Rewarding("I did it! Time to get a candy bar!")

14. *Have persistence. . .*

Persistence is the real key to successful goal achievement. Don't allow yourself to become distracted with excuses for why things can't be done. Excuses are the enemies of goal achievement.

Write down this anonymous piece of classic wisdom and place it where you can read it every day: "Nothing in the world can take the place of persistence. Talent will not: nothing is more common than unsuccessful people with talent. Genius will not: unrewarded genius is almost a proverb. Education will not: the world is full of educated derelicts. Persistence and determination alone are omnipotent."

Invest in a Goal Book

If you are not willing to put your ideas and dreams on paper, you are not willing to achieve them. They must be written down so you can literally see them. Give yourself the opportunity to take your goal book into a quiet place. Out in nature is best, away from phones, kids, and other daily demands. Allow yourself to just relax and become centered. Ask yourself empowering questions such as *What do I really want?* Divide your notebook into twelve or more sections. Start with the area in your life that has the most importance to you and give yourself time to think.

GOAL STARTER IDEAS

1. *Physical*

Ask yourself, in the next year exactly what are you
   going to do to become healthier and in better
   shape?

Exactly what do you want to weigh?

What is the date that you will be your ideal
   weight?

What are you willing to do to reach that weight?

What type foods are you now going to start to eat
   to nurture your body?

What foods are you going to eliminate from your
   diet?

What support system could you use?

What physical exercise will you start?

What sports do you want to learn or improve in
   your performance?

How often and how long will you exercise?

Where will you go to exercise?

With whom could you form a support system to
   keep yourself motivated to exercise?

2. *Family*

What can you do to create a closer more harmonious relationship with your spouse, children,
   parents, in-laws, relatives?

What can you do to be a better role model?

What family activities could you get started to improve your relationships?

How can you reinforce the positive in your
   relationships?

How can you express your love to your family better?

3. *Career or Profession*

How can you improve your level of enjoyment for
   your work?

How can you earn more money or get a promotion?

How can you keep a positive attitude?

What strategies can you use to continue your education and improve your skills?

What professional groups could you join to improve your networking skills?

Are you really happy with this position? If not, where do you really want to be?

4. *Mental or Self-Development*

What type of self-improvement courses will you take?

How many non-fiction books are you going to read this year?

How many audio cassette programs will you invest in this year?

What new skills and procedures will you learn this year?

What programs are you adding to your personal computer?

What lectures are you planning to attend this year?

5. *Financial*

How much are you going to save this year?

How much are you saving for retirement?

How much are you budgeting for your education fund?

What type of investments do you plan to make this year?

How much do you plan to save in five years?

How much do you plan to save in ten years?

6. *Community Support*

What volunteer work are you planning this year?

What civic office or committee could benefit from your time?

How much can you donate of your time and money to worthwhile projects?

7. *Spirituality*

What can you do daily to feel more in touch with the inner you and your creator?

What are you doing to heal yourself emotionally?

8. *Personal Appearance*

What are you going to do to look and feel your very best?

What areas of appearance need attention?

Updating clothes, hair, makeup, personal style?

9. *Free Time and Hobbies*

How much time per week can you devote to play?

When can you schedule play time for yourself and your family and friends?

Where do you want to go on vacation this year?

10. *Stress Management*

How can you reduce your negative stress load?

How can you relax and enjoy your life and your blessings?

How can you create an environment that supports you?

11. *Creativity*

How can you use your creativity to improve the quality of your life?

How can you tap into your creativity to make more money and security for your future?

12. *Personal Relationships*

What can you do that will strengthen your relationships with friends, neighbors, co-workers, and associates?

How can you release all blame, guilt, anger, and grudges toward other people?

How can you show appreciation to your friends more often?

Start Now

Spend one hour fantasizing about what you want your life to look like at the end of this year. Answer all the above questions and add some questions of your own. Write out your answers with as much detail as possible. Setting goals helps you produce specific, measurable, long-lasting changes in yourself. This simple act of getting started will do more for your success than nearly anything else possible. The only true limitation in life is our lack of belief in our own abilities.

The strategy of goal-setting will transform you from being a thinker with good intentions to a doer and achiever. You'll be more motivated, optimistic, and you'll feel more in control of your life than ever before. Your point of power is always in the present. Focus your energies in the direction of your heart's desires. DREAM BIG!

CHAPTER
–18–
THE 21-DAY
SUCCESS FITNESS PLAN

I would like to share with you a story about one of the most important lessons I have ever learned. This lesson has allowed me to focus my life energy in the most efficient manner possible to create a successful life.

I have always liked to think of myself as an adventurer. I love new challenges and I became interested in taking flying lessons. The day of my fourth lesson was very cool and windy; my instructor was letting me fly and I was having a heck of a time keeping the plane on course. I started to become frustrated and began berating myself. My instructor, Mary, listened to me for a few minutes and finally said something very profound: "Lee, when you are flying you must realize that planes do not stay on course very long. It's normal to be off course because of wind shifts. This is not the time to use all your resources to beat yourself up. You need to focus your energy to simply get back on course."

After she made that statement I realized what a wonderful metaphor that was for living. Any time we accidentally veer off our chosen courses, we must remember it's not in our best interest to waste our life energy whipping ourselves. We should just acknowledge what made us stray and use our energy to simply get back on course.

I suggest that you remember this story the next time you find yourself slipping off your exercise program or having to much too eat or drink at a party, or perhaps find yourself losing your temper. So don't waste your precious life energy making yourself feel bad about the past. Remember your goals and purpose, and have enough integrity with yourself that you will get back to your course. Your power is to take action in the present.

Reading or hearing about information will not make you powerful; *taking action* on the information you've *learned, will*! Learning anything new is like learning a sport. When you first try it and for the first few times, you may not be very good, but the more you work with it the better you get. I'm going to ask you to exercise your Success muscles. The following information is a reminder of the mind-set, attitudes, and strategies you can check out for yourself in the next 21 days to improve the quality of your life. By changing your strategies you will produce dramatic new results in your life. Remember that doing anything for 21 days creates a habit. The following strategies are excellent habits to develop for creating a rich life and feeling in control of your destiny.

THE SUCCESSFUL WORKOUT

Start by Making a Variety of Small Changes in Your Life

Don't overwhelm yourself with trying to be perfect and make huge changes in your life style. It's better to build on your confidence with the success of many small changes. A very good strategy to remember is one that Scandinavian Air Systems used to accomplish a major corporate turnaround in just three years. Its president, Jan Carlson, described one of the principles he used with his airline: "We don't seek to be one thousand percent better at any one thing. We seek to be one percent better at one thousand things."

Have Attitude Adjustment Time Every Morning

Before you get out of bed every morning, tell yourself: *Today is going to be a great day! I am going to have fun today. I am going to be resourceful and productive today.*

I am going to be proud of myself today. I am going to be the best I can be, if only for today. The advantages of this kind of self-talk is that you have now programmed your brain for what you want. You're being an actor in life instead of a reactor; you're in charge of the caliber of information that goes into your brain. Nurture yourself daily with books, tapes, and people that make you feel like the worthy human being you are. It's crucial that you love and honor yourself by feeding your soul with positive, uplifting information that allows you to enjoy your life.

Listen To Yourself

Ask yourself empowering questions daily. Pay attention to that small inner voice that so gently guides you into the best direction for yourself. Take action on your instincts. Make time every day to just be alone; allow yourself to relax and center yourself. You must balance your life and pay attention to the inner you, if you want the outer you to be happy and successful. Remember that all success must be created internally before it can manifest externally.

Pay Attention to Your Self-Talk

You *are* a self-fulfilling prophecy. The things you say to yourself are programming what your future will be. You have the power to give yourself the most empowering messages possible. If you don't, who will?

Plug Your Energy Leaks

Do some small task that you've been avoiding. Stop those nagging thoughts that drain you of creative energy. Learn to say "No, thank you" at the appropriate time. Forgive yourself for all past mistakes and forgive all the people who have hurt you. The rewards will be greater than you can imagine, with increased self-esteem and energy to do the things you really want.

Be Flexible

Create a new label for yourself. When you label yourself as easy-going and flexible, you give yourself permission to not let the outside world rule the inside of yourself. Flexibility is power because you will experience less conflict and stress with the world. Another form of flexibility is to let go of your old habits or life ruts. Change your routine for the next 21 days and notice how you start to become more creative. You also give yourself the opportunity to see life from a totally difference perspective when you do things differently. You wake up and become conscious again of how your actions create your future.

Be Unique and Creative

One of the exciting things about success is that you don't always have to follow the rules or take a traditional approach in dealing with life's challenges! As part of your 21-day success fitness plan, I suggest you allow yourself to experiment with new ways to bring about the results you want.

A great example of being creative comes from a friend of my mother's. Ellie is a widow, well-known as a friendly, helpful neighbor. One week a young couple moved into the house next to hers, and Ellie promptly did the neighborly thing. She baked them a cake and, taking it over to their new home, she invited the young couple to come visit and have dinner with her sometime soon. The very next night, as Ellie was about to sit down to dinner, the young couple from next door came over to borrow something. Since they were already there and hadn't eaten, she invited them to stay for dinner. The couple ate with Ellie and then went home.

To Ellie's surprise, the very next night, at the same time, the couple came by again, this time to ask questions about the area. Again Ellie, being a gracious southern lady, invited them to share her evening meal. Well, this became a nightly ritual; the young couple would appear at her doorstep, eat and then leave! Ellie was beside herself; she didn't know what to do—these people expecting her to fix dinner for them every night was too much. And it just wasn't in her manner to not answer the door or to confront them and tell them to not come over to her house. She also felt very uncomfortable with not being hospitable when someone was in her home. All the traditional ways that she knew to stop these people felt too rude and she really didn't want a confrontation.

So Ellie thought and thought and one day came up with a plan. That night when the couple stopped by as usual, as they had for the last two weeks, Ellie had dinner ready. All throughout dinner she talked about this new recipe she was trying out for the local charity bake sale. After dinner the couple usually had some excuse to rush off, but she insisted they stay for dessert. As Ellie cleared the table, she took the dinner dishes and put them on the floor in the kitchen. She then opened the back door and called to her three dogs and two cats; they came running in and started licking all the dinner plates clean. While she talked to her company, the dogs and cats had licked the plates spotless, so Ellie picked them up and began putting them away in the cabinet. She caught only a glimpse of the horror on their faces as they left without even tasting the new cake! They also never showed up for dinner again!

I simply love this story because it's a great example that we can be unique and creative and have fun doing it! You *can* use your own style when dealing with situations in which you must establish your own boundaries of what feels right. You don't have to give your power away to others or old traditions or someone else's rules.

Stop Working so Hard Physically and Start to Use Your Mind

Use your imagination to see yourself performing well in upcoming events. See yourself being successful and enjoying the process. Rehearse your actions in your mind before you try to do them in the physical world. This gives you an edge because it improves your performance and reduces your stress. Mental rehearsal allows you to build your confidence and empowers you to stay motivated.

Create Leverage in Your Life—
Think of Yourself as an Entrepreneur

Even if you are happy in your current position, it's gratifying to create leverage for yourself knowing you have other talents to use if you need them. The Time Line is a powerful exercise because it opens doors to opportunities you probably haven't considered before. Using what you learned by doing Time Line exercises, ask yourself these empowering questions: What can you do to improve your value? What can you do to create more income, benefits, or enjoyment for yourself? What opportunities are in front of you that you could capitalize on for fun and profit?

Nurture Yourself and Count Your Blessings

Give yourself permission to treat yourself with love, kindness, and respect. Take long baths and walks in nature. Read a good book; spend time with your loved ones. All work and no play makes you a dull person. Allow yourself to laugh and have fun! Not only is this strategy healing, it helps your creative side to emerge. Remind yourself how lucky you are and be grateful for all the blessings and joys that you already have. Focus on what is good about yourself and your life. What you focus on determines the quality of life that you experience. If you're seeking more blessings, be thankful for the ones you have now.

Get Clear About What You Want

Spend some quality time alone with yourself and your journal to get specific about what your dreams and goals are. Knowing your purpose is clearly one of the best motivators you can have to excel. Writing out your goals will send a clear message to your subconscious mind on what you want to create with your life energy. You must be able to crystalize your thoughts about what you want to be able to utilize your potential.

Success is Not a Destination—It's a Journey

The past is a locked door. Whatever mistakes or failures you've ever had are truly great tutors for the success you can create in the future. Your past setbacks have been gifts of wisdom; use them wisely. Stay in the present; now is your point of power. Know that the future will take care of itself, if you take care of the present.

Enjoy the Humor of Life

This is one of the most important Success workout exercises you can develop. You have no power over the external world, but you do have power of how it affects you. How much you enjoy your journey is up to you. I'll give you an example from my own life on how important it is to see humor whenever possible; it keeps you sane! One Friday evening, I was preparing to board my flight to come home after working away from home for over a week. I was very excited to be going home because I had a very special engagement to attend that evening. As I sat in this very busy, noisy, crowded airport, the airline representative came on the loudspeaker and announced that our plane was going to be delayed a short time. I was okay with that because it's not unusual. An hour later, the representative announced another hour-long delay and I felt slightly frustrated but was still in a good mood anticipating my wonderful evening when I got home. That hour delay turned into six hours! By this time I had missed the event I had so looked forward to attending, and I was frustrated and angry. At that moment, I had forgotten everything I knew about positive thinking. Then I realized that here I am not walking my own talk; I'm supposed to have integrity with myself, I'm supposed to do the things I teach; so I did a pattern interrupt. I gave myself permission, under the stressful circumstances, to create a foxhole and nurture myself. I went to the nearest coffee shop, sat down, and ordered the biggest piece of chocolate cake they had. As I was enjoying my cake and calming myself down, I noticed a man who had taken the seat next to me. Without doubt, he was one of the biggest nerds on earth. They're easy to spot because those are the guys who wear watches that beep every fifteen minutes to let them know they're alive! And, they like to talk in acronyms.

The waitress approached him and asked, "What would you like?" He looked at her straight-faced and said, "I would like a B-L-T, N-T." Only this waitress was not amused with his request and putting both hands on her hips as she cracked her gum, she said, "Educate me." He replied, "I want a bacon, lettuce and tomato sandwich, not toasted." She brought him the bacon, lettuce and tomato sandwich-not toasted.

Five minutes later, like a good waitress, she came back to check up on the food. She asked, "How is it? He looked at her without hesitating and said, "S-O-B." Her eyes got the size of saucers, and she said, "I beg your pardon!" He replied, "Soggy on the bottom." But I have to admire this woman because at this point she was not about to be outdone. She looked at him and said, "Well, S-H-I-T!" Now his eyes got really big; turning away, she explained, "Should-a had it toasted!"

Your sense of humor is going to get you through many situations over which you have no control. Learn to laugh and remember that you have only 1,440 minutes per day to enjoy this blessing you call life.

Live Life As If You Only Had One Year To Live

Stop putting off enjoying your life; there are no guarantees you'll be here tomorrow! Think of yourself as a leader—your attitude and your behavior effects and mentors the people around you. What positive messages can you be sending out with your behavior daily? Tell the people you love that you love them, send flowers to the living while they can enjoy them! Be nice to yourself and realize that life is too short to sweat the small stuff. It's never money or your material possessions that really make you happy; it's your relationships with others and your self.

Create a Victory Book for Yourself and One of Your Children

Document your past successes. Take time out to pat yourself on the back, to acknowledge your time, energy, and efforts for getting where you are today. Allow yourself to feel good about the lessons you've learned and what you've been able to accomplish. Building confidence strengthens your success muscles. You come to believe in your own ability to reach your dreams.

Learn To Play

Many of us go through life making life tougher than it has to be. Without realizing it, many of us have programmed ourselves not to enjoy our present moment. We bombard our brain with negative, self-defeating messages like *I hate this job, I wish I didn't have to do this, I'm not good at this.* What's the point? You're only programming your brain to not do a good job or to put off even getting started! It's hard to feel motivated toward new projects when you've pre-framed your mind to think they're going to be difficult. I suggest that you stop programming yourself to have a hard life—why not have fun? Why not enjoy the moment? The point is to give your subconscious a new empowering message!

I learned this from one of my mentors, Dini Petty, who is a great inspiration to me. She hosts her own television show, whose theme is "Live, Love and Laugh," which is the number-one-rated talk show in Canada. I believe her show is so highly rated because she is enthusiastic and funny and always leaves people feeling uplifted and good. Dini and her staff of producers decided there was already too much negative television and they wanted to add value to the lives of their viewers with positive subjects.

One thing that I realized has helped make Dini such a tremendous success is that she deliberately programs her mood before being introduced to her live audience. She turns to the staff and producers and announces, "Let's have fun! Let's go PLAY TV!"

Observing her, I saw what a wonderful strategy it is to program your brain to have fun before you do something. Since we are self-fulfilling prophecies, why not honor yourself and set out to enjoy your life? Think about it; when you play, you're having fun, when you're having fun, you're lighthearted, creative, and relaxed. When you allow yourself to have fun, your performance usually improves. It's a Win-Win situation.

After watching Dini Petty consistently do a great job, I decided to check out her strategy and try *playing* at certain tasks that I have in the past considered difficult or unpleasant. The week after I observed Dini's strategy, I had three speaking engagements back-to-back in different cities. This type of trip is usually grueling, but this time I decided to take a new approach. I told myself before I left for the airport that I was going to play vacation traveler; I was going to enjoy the trip. I realized that in the past I had created the feeling of dread because of my attitude of just getting the trip over with. On that occasion, instead of feeling stressed-out, anxious to hurry and get to my destination, I simply kept saying to myself, *I'm a vacation traveler and I have all the time I need.* I can honestly say I was faced with as many obstacles as I normally encounter when traveling, but this trip felt less stressful.

So I decided to try this new strategy out on something I had really avoided. I have tons of research, and much of it gets stacked up around my personal office. I decided to PLAY professional files organizer for just one hour. I tackled the job with the mind-set that it was my most important task at the moment and I was going to enjoy doing it fast and efficiently. As I began organizing my research and filing it away, instead of my usual muttering under my breath, I kept my focus on the fact that I was good at this and the benefits I would enjoy after it was done. To my surprise, I finished faster than I ever had before. Now that I have this new strategy, I don't dread this task any longer. It brings to mind the old saying, "Act the part and you shall become it!"

Food for thought: go "play" whatever role you have to be at the moment. If you are playing golf, be a pro; if you're gardening, be a professional landscaper! Try it; time passes more quickly, you might even have fun and, most importantly, you'll *feel* better about what you're doing.

A Personal Afterword

In closing, I want to congratulate you on your commitment to developing your potential and to learning. Thank you for allowing me to share my experiences and the tools that I use to manifest what I want in life. This book was a process of learning and growing for me. I sincerely pray that you will be inspired to make your life your own living art and create a healthy, happy, and rich life. Today is your opportunity to make a commitment that you are going to really live. You *can* give yourself permission to count your blessings and feel grateful for what you have in life. True wealth is having a passion for living, seeing life as an adventure, loving yourself and others, and making a difference. I challenge you to be the best you can be and share your light with the world. One person *can* make a difference. I would be very touched if you stayed in contact with me. Write to me about your results from feeling your power to create whatever it is that you want. I hope that if our paths cross you'll introduce yourself so I can meet you and hear about your successes.

I leave you with these final words. Your point of power in this lifetime is this moment. Focus your mental, physical, emotional, and spiritual life energy into the direction of what you want to create. Feel your success and you shall manifest it. To change your life all you have to do is feel your power and use it to create whatever riches you want.

God bless you.

Lee Milteer

RESOURCES
For ongoing personal support from Lee Milteer

Coping with Change:
Life Strategies for the '90s
Six Audio Tapes and Workbook $69.95
A powerful program that will help you produce specific, measurable, long-lasting changes in yourself with the information, philosophies, and skills to capitalize on your talents, and create the entrepreneurial spirit for dealing with the future.

Success and Prosperity
90-minute Video $49.95
A 90-minute video presentation that will give you a step-by-step approach to using techniques such as Visualization, Auto-suggestion, and Prosperity Programming.

Ten Strategies for Successful Achievement
Two Audio Tapes $29.95
A two-tape audio program on how to create a positive, successful self-image, increase your learning ability, tap into the creative power of the subconscious mind, and achieve your goals.

How to Break Any Habit in Just 21 Days
Two Audio Tapes $29.95
A two-tape audio program on how to break your worst habit. This tape program will be your coach as you empower yourself to make the changes you desire most for you life.

How to Create Upward Mobility and Success
in Your Career thru Self-Promotion and Publicity.
Single Audio Tape $15.95

How to Make More Money in Real Estate
thru Self-Promotion and Publicity.
Single Audio Tape $15.95

To order or request more information about our programs, please call our office: (804) 460-1818.

Lee Milteer is president of Lee Milteer Associates, Inc. She lives in Virginia Beach, Virginia. Her powerful presentation style has made her one of North America's most highly regarded human potential speakers. Lee is a businesswoman whose background is in sales and management. Since 1980, she has been speaking professionally about success principles to thousands of people throughout the United States, Canada, Great Britain, and the Virgin Islands. Lee is a well-known best-selling audio and video tape author whose products have been endorsed by Nightingale Conant, CareerTrack and SyberVision. She is co-author of the book *Reach Your Career Dreams* and a business columnist for *The Journal of New Thought* magazine. Lee has her own segment as an advice counselor on "The Dini Petty Show," the number-one-rated television talk show in Canada.

If you are interested in a Lee Milteer presentation for your group, please contact her office:

Lee Milteer Associates, Inc., Post Office Box 5653, Virginia Beach, Virginia 23455.
Tel: (804) 460-1818. Fax: (804) 460-3675.